GNU Wget - The non-interactive download utility

A catalogue record for this book is available from the Hong Kong Public Libraries.

Published in Hong Kong by Samurai Media Limited.

Email: info@samuraimedia.org

ISBN 978-988-8381-42-5

Background Cover Image by https://www.flickr.com/people/webtreatsetc/

Table of Contents

1 Overview

GNU Wget is a free utility for non-interactive download of files from the Web. It supports HTTP, HTTPS, and FTP protocols, as well as retrieval through HTTP proxies.

This chapter is a partial overview of Wget's features.

- Wget is non-interactive, meaning that it can work in the background, while the user is not logged on. This allows you to start a retrieval and disconnect from the system, letting Wget finish the work. By contrast, most of the Web browsers require constant user's presence, which can be a great hindrance when transferring a lot of data.

- Wget can follow links in HTML, XHTML, and CSS pages, to create local versions of remote web sites, fully recreating the directory structure of the original site. This is sometimes referred to as "recursive downloading." While doing that, Wget respects the Robot Exclusion Standard (/robots.txt). Wget can be instructed to convert the links in downloaded files to point at the local files, for offline viewing.

- File name wildcard matching and recursive mirroring of directories are available when retrieving via FTP. Wget can read the time-stamp information given by both HTTP and FTP servers, and store it locally. Thus Wget can see if the remote file has changed since last retrieval, and automatically retrieve the new version if it has. This makes Wget suitable for mirroring of FTP sites, as well as home pages.

- Wget has been designed for robustness over slow or unstable network connections; if a download fails due to a network problem, it will keep retrying until the whole file has been retrieved. If the server supports regetting, it will instruct the server to continue the download from where it left off.

- Wget supports proxy servers, which can lighten the network load, speed up retrieval and provide access behind firewalls. Wget uses the passive FTP downloading by default, active FTP being an option.

- Wget supports IP version 6, the next generation of IP. IPv6 is autodetected at compile-time, and can be disabled at either build or run time. Binaries built with IPv6 support work well in both IPv4-only and dual family environments.

- Built-in features offer mechanisms to tune which links you wish to follow (see Chapter 4 [Following Links], page 29).

- The progress of individual downloads is traced using a progress gauge. Interactive downloads are tracked using a "thermometer"-style gauge, whereas non-interactive ones are traced with dots, each dot representing a fixed amount of data received (1KB by default). Either gauge can be customized to your preferences.

- Most of the features are fully configurable, either through command line options, or via the initialization file .wgetrc (see Chapter 6 [Startup File], page 35). Wget allows you to define global startup files (/usr/local/etc/wgetrc by default) for site settings. You can also specify the location of a startup file with the –config option.

- Finally, GNU Wget is free software. This means that everyone may use it, redistribute it and/or modify it under the terms of the GNU General Public License, as published by the Free Software Foundation (see the file COPYING that came with GNU Wget, for details).

2 Invoking

By default, Wget is very simple to invoke. The basic syntax is:

    wget [option]... [URL]...

Wget will simply download all the URLs specified on the command line. *URL* is a *Uniform Resource Locator*, as defined below.

However, you may wish to change some of the default parameters of Wget. You can do it two ways: permanently, adding the appropriate command to `.wgetrc` (see Chapter 6 [Startup File], page 35), or specifying it on the command line.

2.1 URL Format

URL is an acronym for Uniform Resource Locator. A uniform resource locator is a compact string representation for a resource available via the Internet. Wget recognizes the URL syntax as per RFC1738. This is the most widely used form (square brackets denote optional parts):

    http://host[:port]/directory/file
    ftp://host[:port]/directory/file

You can also encode your username and password within a URL:

    ftp://user:password@host/path
    http://user:password@host/path

Either *user* or *password*, or both, may be left out. If you leave out either the HTTP username or password, no authentication will be sent. If you leave out the FTP username, 'anonymous' will be used. If you leave out the FTP password, your email address will be supplied as a default password.[1]

Important Note: if you specify a password-containing URL on the command line, the username and password will be plainly visible to all users on the system, by way of `ps`. On multi-user systems, this is a big security risk. To work around it, use `wget -i -` and feed the URLs to Wget's standard input, each on a separate line, terminated by *C-d*.

You can encode unsafe characters in a URL as '%xy', xy being the hexadecimal representation of the character's ASCII value. Some common unsafe characters include '%' (quoted as '%25'), ':' (quoted as '%3A'), and '@' (quoted as '%40'). Refer to RFC1738 for a comprehensive list of unsafe characters.

Wget also supports the `type` feature for FTP URLs. By default, FTP documents are retrieved in the binary mode (type 'i'), which means that they are downloaded unchanged. Another useful mode is the 'a' (*ASCII*) mode, which converts the line delimiters between the different operating systems, and is thus useful for text files. Here is an example:

    ftp://host/directory/file;type=a

Two alternative variants of URL specification are also supported, because of historical (hysterical?) reasons and their widespreaded use.

FTP-only syntax (supported by NcFTP):

    host:/dir/file

HTTP-only syntax (introduced by Netscape):

    host[:port]/dir/file

These two alternative forms are deprecated, and may cease being supported in the future.

If you do not understand the difference between these notations, or do not know which one to use, just use the plain ordinary format you use with your favorite browser, like Lynx or Netscape.

------

[1] If you have a `.netrc` file in your home directory, password will also be searched for there.

2.2 Option Syntax

Since Wget uses GNU getopt to process command-line arguments, every option has a long form along with the short one. Long options are more convenient to remember, but take time to type. You may freely mix different option styles, or specify options after the command-line arguments. Thus you may write:

        wget -r --tries=10 http://fly.srk.fer.hr/ -o log

The space between the option accepting an argument and the argument may be omitted. Instead of '-o log' you can write '-olog'.

You may put several options that do not require arguments together, like:

        wget -drc URL

This is completely equivalent to:

        wget -d -r -c URL

Since the options can be specified after the arguments, you may terminate them with '--'. So the following will try to download URL '-x', reporting failure to log:

        wget -o log -- -x

The options that accept comma-separated lists all respect the convention that specifying an empty list clears its value. This can be useful to clear the .wgetrc settings. For instance, if your .wgetrc sets exclude_directories to /cgi-bin, the following example will first reset it, and then set it to exclude /~nobody and /~somebody. You can also clear the lists in .wgetrc (see Section 6.2 [Wgetrc Syntax], page 35).

        wget -X '' -X /~nobody,/~somebody

Most options that do not accept arguments are *boolean* options, so named because their state can be captured with a yes-or-no ("boolean") variable. For example, '--follow-ftp' tells Wget to follow FTP links from HTML files and, on the other hand, '--no-glob' tells it not to perform file globbing on FTP URLs. A boolean option is either *affirmative* or *negative* (beginning with '--no'). All such options share several properties.

Unless stated otherwise, it is assumed that the default behavior is the opposite of what the option accomplishes. For example, the documented existence of '--follow-ftp' assumes that the default is to *not* follow FTP links from HTML pages.

Affirmative options can be negated by prepending the '--no-' to the option name; negative options can be negated by omitting the '--no-' prefix. This might seem superfluous—if the default for an affirmative option is to not do something, then why provide a way to explicitly turn it off? But the startup file may in fact change the default. For instance, using follow_ftp = on in .wgetrc makes Wget *follow* FTP links by default, and using '--no-follow-ftp' is the only way to restore the factory default from the command line.

2.3 Basic Startup Options

'-V'
'--version'
        Display the version of Wget.

'-h'
'--help'   Print a help message describing all of Wget's command-line options.

'-b'
'--background'
        Go to background immediately after startup. If no output file is specified via the
        '-o', output is redirected to wget-log.

'-e *command*'
'--execute *command*'

> Execute *command* as if it were a part of .wgetrc (see Chapter 6 [Startup File], page 35). A command thus invoked will be executed *after* the commands in .wgetrc, thus taking precedence over them. If you need to specify more than one wgetrc command, use multiple instances of '-e'.

2.4 Logging and Input File Options

'-o *logfile*'
'--output-file=*logfile*'

> Log all messages to *logfile*. The messages are normally reported to standard error.

'-a *logfile*'
'--append-output=*logfile*'

> Append to *logfile*. This is the same as '-o', only it appends to *logfile* instead of overwriting the old log file. If *logfile* does not exist, a new file is created.

'-d'
'--debug'   Turn on debug output, meaning various information important to the developers of Wget if it does not work properly. Your system administrator may have chosen to compile Wget without debug support, in which case '-d' will not work. Please note that compiling with debug support is always safe—Wget compiled with the debug support will *not* print any debug info unless requested with '-d'. See Section 8.6 [Reporting Bugs], page 50, for more information on how to use '-d' for sending bug reports.

'-q'
'--quiet'   Turn off Wget's output.

'-v'
'--verbose'

> Turn on verbose output, with all the available data. The default output is verbose.

'-nv'
'--no-verbose'

> Turn off verbose without being completely quiet (use '-q' for that), which means that error messages and basic information still get printed.

'--report-speed=*type*'

> Output bandwidth as *type*. The only accepted value is 'bits'.

'-i *file*'
'--input-file=*file*'

> Read URLs from a local or external *file*. If '-' is specified as *file*, URLs are read from the standard input. (Use './-' to read from a file literally named '-'.)

> If this function is used, no URLs need be present on the command line. If there are URLs both on the command line and in an input file, those on the command lines will be the first ones to be retrieved. If '--force-html' is not specified, then *file* should consist of a series of URLs, one per line.

> However, if you specify '--force-html', the document will be regarded as 'html'. In that case you may have problems with relative links, which you can solve either by adding <base href="url"> to the documents or by specifying '--base=*url*' on the command line.

If the *file* is an external one, the document will be automatically treated as 'html' if the Content-Type matches 'text/html'. Furthermore, the *file*'s location will be implicitly used as base href if none was specified.

'-F'

'--force-html'

When input is read from a file, force it to be treated as an HTML file. This enables you to retrieve relative links from existing HTML files on your local disk, by adding `<base href="url">` to HTML, or using the '--base' command-line option.

'-B *URL*'

'--base=*URL*'

Resolves relative links using *URL* as the point of reference, when reading links from an HTML file specified via the '-i'/'--input-file' option (together with '--force-html', or when the input file was fetched remotely from a server describing it as HTML). This is equivalent to the presence of a BASE tag in the HTML input file, with *URL* as the value for the href attribute.

For instance, if you specify 'http://foo/bar/a.html' for *URL*, and Wget reads '../baz/b.html' from the input file, it would be resolved to 'http://foo/baz/b.html'.

'--config=*FILE*'

Specify the location of a startup file you wish to use.

2.5 Download Options

'--bind-address=*ADDRESS*'

When making client TCP/IP connections, bind to *ADDRESS* on the local machine. *ADDRESS* may be specified as a hostname or IP address. This option can be useful if your machine is bound to multiple IPs.

'-t *number*'

'--tries=*number*'

Set number of tries to *number*. Specify 0 or 'inf' for infinite retrying. The default is to retry 20 times, with the exception of fatal errors like "connection refused" or "not found" (404), which are not retried.

'-O *file*'

'--output-document=*file*'

The documents will not be written to the appropriate files, but all will be concatenated together and written to *file*. If ' ' is used as *file*, documents will be printed to standard output, disabling link conversion. (Use './-' to print to a file literally named '-'.)

Use of '-O' is *not* intended to mean simply "use the name *file* instead of the one in the URL;" rather, it is analogous to shell redirection: 'wget -O file http://foo' is intended to work like 'wget -O - http://foo > file'; file will be truncated immediately, and *all* downloaded content will be written there.

For this reason, '-N' (for timestamp-checking) is not supported in combination with '-O': since *file* is always newly created, it will always have a very new timestamp. A warning will be issued if this combination is used.

Similarly, using '-r' or '-p' with '-O' may not work as you expect: Wget won't just download the first file to *file* and then download the rest to their normal names: *all* downloaded content will be placed in *file*. This was disabled in version 1.11, but has been reinstated (with a warning) in 1.11.2, as there are some cases where this behavior can actually have some use.

Note that a combination with '-k' is only permitted when downloading a single document, as in that case it will just convert all relative URIs to external ones; '-k' makes no sense for multiple URIs when they're all being downloaded to a single file; '-k' can be used only when the output is a regular file.

'-nc'
'--no-clobber'

> If a file is downloaded more than once in the same directory, Wget's behavior depends on a few options, including '-nc'. In certain cases, the local file will be *clobbered*, or overwritten, upon repeated download. In other cases it will be preserved.
>
> When running Wget without '-N', '-nc', '-r', or '-p', downloading the same file in the same directory will result in the original copy of *file* being preserved and the second copy being named '*file.1*'. If that file is downloaded yet again, the third copy will be named '*file.2*', and so on. (This is also the behavior with '-nd', even if '-r' or '-p' are in effect.) When '-nc' is specified, this behavior is suppressed, and Wget will refuse to download newer copies of '*file*'. Therefore, "no-clobber" is actually a misnomer in this mode—it's not clobbering that's prevented (as the numeric suffixes were already preventing clobbering), but rather the multiple version saving that's prevented.
>
> When running Wget with '-r' or '-p', but without '-N', '-nd', or '-nc', redownloading a file will result in the new copy simply overwriting the old. Adding '-nc' will prevent this behavior, instead causing the original version to be preserved and any newer copies on the server to be ignored.
>
> When running Wget with '-N', with or without '-r' or '-p', the decision as to whether or not to download a newer copy of a file depends on the local and remote timestamp and size of the file (see Chapter 5 [Time-Stamping], page 33). '-nc' may not be specified at the same time as '-N'.
>
> Note that when '-nc' is specified, files with the suffixes '.html' or '.htm' will be loaded from the local disk and parsed as if they had been retrieved from the Web.

'--backups=*backups*'

> Before (over)writing a file, back up an existing file by adding a '.1' suffix ('_1' on VMS) to the file name. Such backup files are rotated to '.2', '.3', and so on, up to *backups* (and lost beyond that).

'-c'
'--continue'

> Continue getting a partially-downloaded file. This is useful when you want to finish up a download started by a previous instance of Wget, or by another program. For instance:
>
>   wget -c ftp://sunsite.doc.ic.ac.uk/ls-lR.Z
>
> If there is a file named ls-lR.Z in the current directory, Wget will assume that it is the first portion of the remote file, and will ask the server to continue the retrieval from an offset equal to the length of the local file.
>
> Note that you don't need to specify this option if you just want the current invocation of Wget to retry downloading a file should the connection be lost midway through. This is the default behavior. '-c' only affects resumption of downloads started *prior* to this invocation of Wget, and whose local files are still sitting around.

Without '-c', the previous example would just download the remote file to `ls-lR.Z.1`, leaving the truncated `ls-lR.Z` file alone.

Beginning with Wget 1.7, if you use '-c' on a non-empty file, and it turns out that the server does not support continued downloading, Wget will refuse to start the download from scratch, which would effectively ruin existing contents. If you really want the download to start from scratch, remove the file.

Also beginning with Wget 1.7, if you use '-c' on a file which is of equal size as the one on the server, Wget will refuse to download the file and print an explanatory message. The same happens when the file is smaller on the server than locally (presumably because it was changed on the server since your last download attempt)—because "continuing" is not meaningful, no download occurs.

On the other side of the coin, while using '-c', any file that's bigger on the server than locally will be considered an incomplete download and only (`length(remote) - length(local)`) bytes will be downloaded and tacked onto the end of the local file. This behavior can be desirable in certain cases—for instance, you can use '`wget -c`' to download just the new portion that's been appended to a data collection or log file.

However, if the file is bigger on the server because it's been *changed*, as opposed to just *appended* to, you'll end up with a garbled file. Wget has no way of verifying that the local file is really a valid prefix of the remote file. You need to be especially careful of this when using '-c' in conjunction with '-r', since every file will be considered as an "incomplete download" candidate.

Another instance where you'll get a garbled file if you try to use '-c' is if you have a lame HTTP proxy that inserts a "transfer interrupted" string into the local file. In the future a "rollback" option may be added to deal with this case.

Note that '-c' only works with FTP servers and with HTTP servers that support the `Range` header.

'`--start-pos=OFFSET`'

Start downloading at zero-based position *OFFSET*. Offset may be expressed in bytes, kilobytes with the 'k' suffix, or megabytes with the 'm' suffix, etc.

'`--start-pos`' has higher precedence over '`--continue`'. When '`--start-pos`' and '`--continue`' are both specified, wget will emit a warning then proceed as if '`--continue`' was absent.

Server support for continued download is required, otherwise '`--start-pos`' cannot help. See '-c' for details.

'`--progress=type`'

Select the type of the progress indicator you wish to use. Legal indicators are "dot" and "bar".

The "bar" indicator is used by default. It draws an ASCII progress bar graphics (a.k.a "thermometer" display) indicating the status of retrieval. If the output is not a TTY, the "dot" bar will be used by default.

Use '`--progress=dot`' to switch to the "dot" display. It traces the retrieval by printing dots on the screen, each dot representing a fixed amount of downloaded data.

The progress *type* can also take one or more parameters. The parameters vary based on the *type* selected. Parameters to *type* are passed by appending them to the type sperated by a colon (:) like this: '`--progress=type:parameter1:parameter2`'.

When using the dotted retrieval, you may set the *style* by specifying the type as '`dot:style`'. Different styles assign different meaning to one dot. With the `default` style each dot represents 1K, there are ten dots in a cluster and 50 dots in a line. The `binary` style has a more "computer"-like orientation—8K dots, 16-dots clusters and 48 dots per line (which makes for 384K lines). The `mega` style is suitable for downloading large files—each dot represents 64K retrieved, there are eight dots in a cluster, and 48 dots on each line (so each line contains 3M). If `mega` is not enough then you can use the `giga` style—each dot represents 1M retrieved, there are eight dots in a cluster, and 32 dots on each line (so each line contains 32M).

With '`--progress=bar`', there are currently two possible parameters, *force* and *noscroll*.

When the output is not a TTY, the progress bar always falls back to "dot", even if '`--progress=bar`' was passed to Wget during invokation. This behaviour can be overridden and the "bar" output forced by using the "force" parameter as '`--progress=bar:force`'.

By default, the '`bar`' style progress bar scroll the name of the file from left to right for the file being downloaded if the filename exceeds the maximum length allotted for its display. In certain cases, such as with '`--progress=bar:force`', one may not want the scrolling filename in the progress bar. By passing the "noscroll" parameter, Wget can be forced to display as much of the filename as possible without scrolling through it.

Note that you can set the default style using the `progress` command in `.wgetrc`. That setting may be overridden from the command line. For example, to force the bar output without scrolling, use '`--progress=bar:force:noscroll`'.

'`--show-progress`'

Force wget to display the progress bar in any verbosity.

By default, wget only displays the progress bar in verbose mode. One may however, want wget to display the progress bar on screen in conjunction with any other verbosity modes like '`--no-verbose`' or '`--quiet`'. This is often a desired a property when invoking wget to download several small/large files. In such a case, wget could simply be invoked with this parameter to get a much cleaner output on the screen.

This option will also force the progress bar to be printed to `stderr` when used alongside the '`--logfile`' option.

'`-N`'
'`--timestamping`'

Turn on time-stamping. See Chapter 5 [Time-Stamping], page 33, for details.

'`--no-use-server-timestamps`'

Don't set the local file's timestamp by the one on the server.

By default, when a file is downloaded, its timestamps are set to match those from the remote file. This allows the use of '`--timestamping`' on subsequent invocations of wget. However, it is sometimes useful to base the local file's timestamp on when it was actually downloaded; for that purpose, the '`--no-use-server-timestamps`' option has been provided.

'`-S`'
'`--server-response`'

Print the headers sent by HTTP servers and responses sent by FTP servers.

'`--spider`'

When invoked with this option, Wget will behave as a Web *spider*, which means that it will not download the pages, just check that they are there. For example, you can use Wget to check your bookmarks:

```
wget --spider --force-html -i bookmarks.html
```

This feature needs much more work for Wget to get close to the functionality of real web spiders.

'-T seconds'
'--timeout=seconds'

Set the network timeout to seconds seconds. This is equivalent to specifying '--dns-timeout', '--connect-timeout', and '--read-timeout', all at the same time.

When interacting with the network, Wget can check for timeout and abort the operation if it takes too long. This prevents anomalies like hanging reads and infinite connects. The only timeout enabled by default is a 900-second read timeout. Setting a timeout to 0 disables it altogether. Unless you know what you are doing, it is best not to change the default timeout settings.

All timeout-related options accept decimal values, as well as subsecond values. For example, '0.1' seconds is a legal (though unwise) choice of timeout. Subsecond timeouts are useful for checking server response times or for testing network latency.

'--dns-timeout=seconds'

Set the DNS lookup timeout to seconds seconds. DNS lookups that don't complete within the specified time will fail. By default, there is no timeout on DNS lookups, other than that implemented by system libraries.

'--connect-timeout=seconds'

Set the connect timeout to seconds seconds. TCP connections that take longer to establish will be aborted. By default, there is no connect timeout, other than that implemented by system libraries.

'--read-timeout=seconds'

Set the read (and write) timeout to seconds seconds. The "time" of this timeout refers to idle time: if, at any point in the download, no data is received for more than the specified number of seconds, reading fails and the download is restarted. This option does not directly affect the duration of the entire download.

Of course, the remote server may choose to terminate the connection sooner than this option requires. The default read timeout is 900 seconds.

'--limit-rate=amount'

Limit the download speed to amount bytes per second. Amount may be expressed in bytes, kilobytes with the 'k' suffix, or megabytes with the 'm' suffix. For example, '--limit-rate=20k' will limit the retrieval rate to 20KB/s. This is useful when, for whatever reason, you don't want Wget to consume the entire available bandwidth.

This option allows the use of decimal numbers, usually in conjunction with power suffixes; for example, '--limit-rate=2.5k' is a legal value.

Note that Wget implements the limiting by sleeping the appropriate amount of time after a network read that took less time than specified by the rate. Eventually this strategy causes the TCP transfer to slow down to approximately the specified rate. However, it may take some time for this balance to be achieved, so don't be surprised if limiting the rate doesn't work well with very small files.

'-w seconds'
'--wait=seconds'

Wait the specified number of seconds between the retrievals. Use of this option is recommended, as it lightens the server load by making the requests less frequent.

Instead of in seconds, the time can be specified in minutes using the m suffix, in hours using h suffix, or in days using d suffix.

Specifying a large value for this option is useful if the network or the destination host is down, so that Wget can wait long enough to reasonably expect the network error to be fixed before the retry. The waiting interval specified by this function is influenced by `--random-wait`, which see.

'`--waitretry=seconds`'

If you don't want Wget to wait between *every* retrieval, but only between retries of failed downloads, you can use this option. Wget will use *linear backoff*, waiting 1 second after the first failure on a given file, then waiting 2 seconds after the second failure on that file, up to the maximum number of *seconds* you specify.

By default, Wget will assume a value of 10 seconds.

'`--random-wait`'

Some web sites may perform log analysis to identify retrieval programs such as Wget by looking for statistically significant similarities in the time between requests. This option causes the time between requests to vary between 0.5 and 1.5 * *wait* seconds, where *wait* was specified using the '`--wait`' option, in order to mask Wget's presence from such analysis.

A 2001 article in a publication devoted to development on a popular consumer platform provided code to perform this analysis on the fly. Its author suggested blocking at the class C address level to ensure automated retrieval programs were blocked despite changing DHCP-supplied addresses.

The '`--random-wait`' option was inspired by this ill-advised recommendation to block many unrelated users from a web site due to the actions of one.

'`--no-proxy`'

Don't use proxies, even if the appropriate `*_proxy` environment variable is defined.

See Section 8.1 [Proxies], page 49, for more information about the use of proxies with Wget.

'`-Q quota`'
'`--quota=quota`'

Specify download quota for automatic retrievals. The value can be specified in bytes (default), kilobytes (with 'k' suffix), or megabytes (with 'm' suffix).

Note that quota will never affect downloading a single file. So if you specify '`wget -Q10k ftp://wuarchive.wustl.edu/ls-lR.gz`', all of the `ls-lR.gz` will be downloaded. The same goes even when several URLs are specified on the command-line. However, quota is respected when retrieving either recursively, or from an input file. Thus you may safely type '`wget -Q2m -i sites`'—download will be aborted when the quota is exceeded.

Setting quota to 0 or to '`inf`' unlimits the download quota.

'`--no-dns-cache`'

Turn off caching of DNS lookups. Normally, Wget remembers the IP addresses it looked up from DNS so it doesn't have to repeatedly contact the DNS server for the same (typically small) set of hosts it retrieves from. This cache exists in memory only; a new Wget run will contact DNS again.

However, it has been reported that in some situations it is not desirable to cache host names, even for the duration of a short-running application like Wget. With this option Wget issues a new DNS lookup (more precisely, a new call to `gethostbyname` or `getaddrinfo`) each time it makes a new connection. Please note that this option will *not* affect caching that might be performed by the resolving library or by an external caching layer, such as NSCD.

If you don't understand exactly what this option does, you probably won't need it.

'`--restrict-file-names=`*modes*'

> Change which characters found in remote URLs must be escaped during generation of local filenames. Characters that are *restricted* by this option are escaped, i.e. replaced with '`%HH`', where '`HH`' is the hexadecimal number that corresponds to the restricted character. This option may also be used to force all alphabetical cases to be either lower- or uppercase.
>
> By default, Wget escapes the characters that are not valid or safe as part of file names on your operating system, as well as control characters that are typically unprintable. This option is useful for changing these defaults, perhaps because you are downloading to a non-native partition, or because you want to disable escaping of the control characters, or you want to further restrict characters to only those in the ASCII range of values.
>
> The *modes* are a comma-separated set of text values. The acceptable values are '`unix`', '`windows`', '`nocontrol`', '`ascii`', '`lowercase`', and '`uppercase`'. The values '`unix`' and '`windows`' are mutually exclusive (one will override the other), as are '`lowercase`' and '`uppercase`'. Those last are special cases, as they do not change the set of characters that would be escaped, but rather force local file paths to be converted either to lower- or uppercase.
>
> When "unix" is specified, Wget escapes the character '/' and the control characters in the ranges 0–31 and 128–159. This is the default on Unix-like operating systems.
>
> When "windows" is given, Wget escapes the characters '\', '|', '/', ':', '?', '"', '*', '<', '>', and the control characters in the ranges 0–31 and 128–159. In addition to this, Wget in Windows mode uses '+' instead of ':' to separate host and port in local file names, and uses '@' instead of '?' to separate the query portion of the file name from the rest. Therefore, a URL that would be saved as '`www.xemacs.org:4300/search.pl?input=blah`' in Unix mode would be saved as '`www.xemacs.org+4300/search.pl@input=blah`' in Windows mode. This mode is the default on Windows.
>
> If you specify '`nocontrol`', then the escaping of the control characters is also switched off. This option may make sense when you are downloading URLs whose names contain UTF-8 characters, on a system which can save and display filenames in UTF-8 (some possible byte values used in UTF-8 byte sequences fall in the range of values designated by Wget as "controls").
>
> The '`ascii`' mode is used to specify that any bytes whose values are outside the range of ASCII characters (that is, greater than 127) shall be escaped. This can be useful when saving filenames whose encoding does not match the one used locally.

'`-4`'
'`--inet4-only`'
'`-6`'
'`--inet6-only`'

> Force connecting to IPv4 or IPv6 addresses. With '`--inet4-only`' or '`-4`', Wget will only connect to IPv4 hosts, ignoring AAAA records in DNS, and refusing to connect to IPv6 addresses specified in URLs. Conversely, with '`--inet6-only`' or '`-6`', Wget will only connect to IPv6 hosts and ignore A records and IPv4 addresses.
>
> Neither options should be needed normally. By default, an IPv6-aware Wget will use the address family specified by the host's DNS record. If the DNS responds with

both IPv4 and IPv6 addresses, Wget will try them in sequence until it finds one it can connect to. (Also see `--prefer-family` option described below.)

These options can be used to deliberately force the use of IPv4 or IPv6 address families on dual family systems, usually to aid debugging or to deal with broken network configuration. Only one of '`--inet6-only`' and '`--inet4-only`' may be specified at the same time. Neither option is available in Wget compiled without IPv6 support.

'`--prefer-family=none/IPv4/IPv6`'

When given a choice of several addresses, connect to the addresses with specified address family first. The address order returned by DNS is used without change by default.

This avoids spurious errors and connect attempts when accessing hosts that resolve to both IPv6 and IPv4 addresses from IPv4 networks. For example, '`www.kame.net`' resolves to '`2001:200:0:8002:203:47ff:fea5:3085`' and to '`203.178.141.194`'. When the preferred family is `IPv4`, the IPv4 address is used first; when the preferred family is `IPv6`, the IPv6 address is used first; if the specified value is `none`, the address order returned by DNS is used without change.

Unlike '`-4`' and '`-6`', this option doesn't inhibit access to any address family, it only changes the *order* in which the addresses are accessed. Also note that the reordering performed by this option is *stable*—it doesn't affect order of addresses of the same family. That is, the relative order of all IPv4 addresses and of all IPv6 addresses remains intact in all cases.

'`--retry-connrefused`'

Consider "connection refused" a transient error and try again. Normally Wget gives up on a URL when it is unable to connect to the site because failure to connect is taken as a sign that the server is not running at all and that retries would not help. This option is for mirroring unreliable sites whose servers tend to disappear for short periods of time.

'`--user=user`'
'`--password=password`'

Specify the username *user* and password *password* for both FTP and HTTP file retrieval. These parameters can be overridden using the '`--ftp-user`' and '`--ftp-password`' options for FTP connections and the '`--http-user`' and '`--http-password`' options for HTTP connections.

'`--ask-password`'

Prompt for a password for each connection established. Cannot be specified when '`--password`' is being used, because they are mutually exclusive.

'`--no-iri`'

Turn off internationalized URI (IRI) support. Use '`--iri`' to turn it on. IRI support is activated by default.

You can set the default state of IRI support using the `iri` command in `.wgetrc`. That setting may be overridden from the command line.

'`--local-encoding=encoding`'

Force Wget to use *encoding* as the default system encoding. That affects how Wget converts URLs specified as arguments from locale to UTF-8 for IRI support.

Wget use the function `nl_langinfo()` and then the `CHARSET` environment variable to get the locale. If it fails, ASCII is used.

You can set the default local encoding using the `local_encoding` command in `.wgetrc`. That setting may be overridden from the command line.

'`--remote-encoding=`*encoding*'

> Force Wget to use *encoding* as the default remote server encoding. That affects how Wget converts URIs found in files from remote encoding to UTF-8 during a recursive fetch. This options is only useful for IRI support, for the interpretation of non-ASCII characters.
>
> For HTTP, remote encoding can be found in HTTP `Content-Type` header and in HTML `Content-Type` `http-equiv` meta tag.
>
> You can set the default encoding using the `remoteencoding` command in `.wgetrc`. That setting may be overridden from the command line.

'`--unlink`'

> Force Wget to unlink file instead of clobbering existing file. This option is useful for downloading to the directory with hardlinks.

2.6 Directory Options

'`-nd`'
'`--no-directories`'

> Do not create a hierarchy of directories when retrieving recursively. With this option turned on, all files will get saved to the current directory, without clobbering (if a name shows up more than once, the filenames will get extensions '`.n`').

'`-x`'
'`--force-directories`'

> The opposite of '`-nd`'—create a hierarchy of directories, even if one would not have been created otherwise. E.g. '`wget -x http://fly.srk.fer.hr/robots.txt`' will save the downloaded file to `fly.srk.fer.hr/robots.txt`.

'`-nH`'
'`--no-host-directories`'

> Disable generation of host-prefixed directories. By default, invoking Wget with '`-r http://fly.srk.fer.hr/`' will create a structure of directories beginning with `fly.srk.fer.hr/`. This option disables such behavior.

'`--protocol-directories`'

> Use the protocol name as a directory component of local file names. For example, with this option, '`wget -r http://`*host*' will save to '`http/`*host*`/...`' rather than just to '*host*`/...`'.

'`--cut-dirs=`*number*'

> Ignore *number* directory components. This is useful for getting a fine-grained control over the directory where recursive retrieval will be saved.
>
> Take, for example, the directory at '`ftp://ftp.xemacs.org/pub/xemacs/`'. If you retrieve it with '`-r`', it will be saved locally under `ftp.xemacs.org/pub/xemacs/`. While the '`-nH`' option can remove the `ftp.xemacs.org/` part, you are still stuck with `pub/xemacs`. This is where '`--cut-dirs`' comes in handy; it makes Wget not "see" *number* remote directory components. Here are several examples of how '`--cut-dirs`' option works.

```
            No options          -> ftp.xemacs.org/pub/xemacs/
            -nH                 -> pub/xemacs/
            -nH --cut-dirs=1    -> xemacs/
            -nH --cut-dirs=2    -> .

            --cut-dirs=1        -> ftp.xemacs.org/xemacs/
            ...
```

If you just want to get rid of the directory structure, this option is similar to a combination of '-nd' and '-P'. However, unlike '-nd', '--cut-dirs' does not lose with subdirectories—for instance, with '-nH --cut-dirs=1', a beta/ subdirectory will be placed to xemacs/beta, as one would expect.

'-P prefix'
'--directory-prefix=prefix'

Set directory prefix to prefix. The directory prefix is the directory where all other files and subdirectories will be saved to, i.e. the top of the retrieval tree. The default is '.' (the current directory).

2.7 HTTP Options

'--default-page=name'

Use name as the default file name when it isn't known (i.e., for URLs that end in a slash), instead of index.html.

'-E'
'--adjust-extension'

If a file of type 'application/xhtml+xml' or 'text/html' is downloaded and the URL does not end with the regexp '\.[Hh][Tt][Mm][Ll]?', this option will cause the suffix '.html' to be appended to the local filename. This is useful, for instance, when you're mirroring a remote site that uses '.asp' pages, but you want the mirrored pages to be viewable on your stock Apache server. Another good use for this is when you're downloading CGI-generated materials. A URL like 'http://site.com/article.cgi?25' will be saved as article.cgi?25.html.

Note that filenames changed in this way will be re-downloaded every time you re-mirror a site, because Wget can't tell that the local X.html file corresponds to remote URL 'X' (since it doesn't yet know that the URL produces output of type 'text/html' or 'application/xhtml+xml'.

As of version 1.12, Wget will also ensure that any downloaded files of type 'text/css' end in the suffix '.css', and the option was renamed from '--html-extension', to better reflect its new behavior. The old option name is still acceptable, but should now be considered deprecated.

At some point in the future, this option may well be expanded to include suffixes for other types of content, including content types that are not parsed by Wget.

'--http-user=user'
'--http-password=password'

Specify the username user and password password on an HTTP server. According to the type of the challenge, Wget will encode them using either the basic (insecure), the digest, or the Windows NTLM authentication scheme.

Another way to specify username and password is in the URL itself (see Section 2.1 [URL Format], page 2). Either method reveals your password to anyone who bothers to run ps. To prevent the passwords from being seen, store them in .wgetrc or .netrc, and make sure to protect those files from other users with chmod. If the passwords are really important, do not leave them lying in those files either—edit the files and delete them after Wget has started the download.

See Section 9.2 [Security Considerations], page 54, for more information about security issues with Wget.

'--no-http-keep-alive'

Turn off the "keep-alive" feature for HTTP downloads. Normally, Wget asks the server to keep the connection open so that, when you download more than one document from the same server, they get transferred over the same TCP connection. This saves time and at the same time reduces the load on the server.

This option is useful when, for some reason, persistent (keep-alive) connections don't work for you, for example due to a server bug or due to the inability of server-side scripts to cope with the connections.

'--no-cache'

Disable server-side cache. In this case, Wget will send the remote server an appropriate directive ('Pragma: no-cache') to get the file from the remote service, rather than returning the cached version. This is especially useful for retrieving and flushing out-of-date documents on proxy servers.

Caching is allowed by default.

'--no-cookies'

Disable the use of cookies. Cookies are a mechanism for maintaining server-side state. The server sends the client a cookie using the Set-Cookie header, and the client responds with the same cookie upon further requests. Since cookies allow the server owners to keep track of visitors and for sites to exchange this information, some consider them a breach of privacy. The default is to use cookies; however, *storing* cookies is not on by default.

'--load-cookies *file*'

Load cookies from *file* before the first HTTP retrieval. *file* is a textual file in the format originally used by Netscape's cookies.txt file.

You will typically use this option when mirroring sites that require that you be logged in to access some or all of their content. The login process typically works by the web server issuing an HTTP cookie upon receiving and verifying your credentials. The cookie is then resent by the browser when accessing that part of the site, and so proves your identity.

Mirroring such a site requires Wget to send the same cookies your browser sends when communicating with the site. This is achieved by '--load-cookies'—simply point Wget to the location of the cookies.txt file, and it will send the same cookies your browser would send in the same situation. Different browsers keep textual cookie files in different locations:

Netscape 4.x.
        The cookies are in ~/.netscape/cookies.txt.

Mozilla and Netscape 6.x.
        Mozilla's cookie file is also named cookies.txt, located somewhere under ~/.mozilla, in the directory of your profile. The full path usually ends up looking somewhat like ~/.mozilla/default/*some-weird-string*/cookies.txt.

Internet Explorer.
        You can produce a cookie file Wget can use by using the File menu, Import and Export, Export Cookies. This has been tested with Internet Explorer 5; it is not guaranteed to work with earlier versions.

Other browsers.
        If you are using a different browser to create your cookies, '--load-cookies' will only work if you can locate or produce a cookie file in the Netscape format that Wget expects.

If you cannot use '--load-cookies', there might still be an alternative. If your browser supports a "cookie manager", you can use it to view the cookies used when accessing the site you're mirroring. Write down the name and value of the cookie, and manually instruct Wget to send those cookies, bypassing the "official" cookie support:

```
wget --no-cookies --header "Cookie: name=value"
```

`--save-cookies file`

> Save cookies to *file* before exiting. This will not save cookies that have expired or that have no expiry time (so-called "session cookies"), but also see `--keep-session-cookies`.

`--keep-session-cookies`

> When specified, causes `--save-cookies` to also save session cookies. Session cookies are normally not saved because they are meant to be kept in memory and forgotten when you exit the browser. Saving them is useful on sites that require you to log in or to visit the home page before you can access some pages. With this option, multiple Wget runs are considered a single browser session as far as the site is concerned.
>
> Since the cookie file format does not normally carry session cookies, Wget marks them with an expiry timestamp of 0. Wget's `--load-cookies` recognizes those as session cookies, but it might confuse other browsers. Also note that cookies so loaded will be treated as other session cookies, which means that if you want `--save-cookies` to preserve them again, you must use `--keep-session-cookies` again.

`--ignore-length`

> Unfortunately, some HTTP servers (CGI programs, to be more precise) send out bogus `Content-Length` headers, which makes Wget go wild, as it thinks not all the document was retrieved. You can spot this syndrome if Wget retries getting the same document again and again, each time claiming that the (otherwise normal) connection has closed on the very same byte.
>
> With this option, Wget will ignore the `Content-Length` header—as if it never existed.

`--header=header-line`

> Send *header-line* along with the rest of the headers in each HTTP request. The supplied header is sent as-is, which means it must contain name and value separated by colon, and must not contain newlines.
>
> You may define more than one additional header by specifying `--header` more than once.

```
wget --header='Accept-Charset: iso-8859-2' \
     --header='Accept-Language: hr'         \
       http://fly.srk.fer.hr/
```

> Specification of an empty string as the header value will clear all previous user-defined headers.
>
> As of Wget 1.10, this option can be used to override headers otherwise generated automatically. This example instructs Wget to connect to localhost, but to specify `foo.bar` in the `Host` header:

```
wget --header="Host: foo.bar" http://localhost/
```

> In versions of Wget prior to 1.10 such use of `--header` caused sending of duplicate headers.

'`--max-redirect=`*number*'

>   Specifies the maximum number of redirections to follow for a resource. The default is 20, which is usually far more than necessary. However, on those occasions where you want to allow more (or fewer), this is the option to use.

'`--proxy-user=`*user*'
'`--proxy-password=`*password*'

>   Specify the username *user* and password *password* for authentication on a proxy server. Wget will encode them using the `basic` authentication scheme.
>
>   Security considerations similar to those with '`--http-password`' pertain here as well.

'`--referer=`*url*'

>   Include 'Referer: *url*' header in HTTP request. Useful for retrieving documents with server-side processing that assume they are always being retrieved by interactive web browsers and only come out properly when Referer is set to one of the pages that point to them.

'`--save-headers`'

>   Save the headers sent by the HTTP server to the file, preceding the actual contents, with an empty line as the separator.

'`-U` *agent-string*'
'`--user-agent=`*agent-string*'

>   Identify as *agent-string* to the HTTP server.
>
>   The HTTP protocol allows the clients to identify themselves using a `User-Agent` header field. This enables distinguishing the WWW software, usually for statistical purposes or for tracing of protocol violations. Wget normally identifies as '`Wget/`*version*', *version* being the current version number of Wget.
>
>   However, some sites have been known to impose the policy of tailoring the output according to the `User-Agent`-supplied information. While this is not such a bad idea in theory, it has been abused by servers denying information to clients other than (historically) Netscape or, more frequently, Microsoft Internet Explorer. This option allows you to change the `User-Agent` line issued by Wget. Use of this option is discouraged, unless you really know what you are doing.
>
>   Specifying empty user agent with '`--user-agent=""`' instructs Wget not to send the `User-Agent` header in HTTP requests.

'`--post-data=`*string*'
'`--post-file=`*file*'

>   Use POST as the method for all HTTP requests and send the specified data in the request body. '`--post-data`' sends *string* as data, whereas '`--post-file`' sends the contents of *file*. Other than that, they work in exactly the same way. In particular, they *both* expect content of the form `key1=value1&key2=value2`, with percent-encoding for special characters; the only difference is that one expects its content as a command-line parameter and the other accepts its content from a file. In particular, '`--post-file`' is *not* for transmitting files as form attachments: those must appear as `key=value` data (with appropriate percent-coding) just like everything else. Wget does not currently support `multipart/form-data` for transmitting POST data; only `application/x-www-form-urlencoded`. Only one of '`--post-data`' and '`--post-file`' should be specified.
>
>   Please note that wget does not require the content to be of the form `key1=value1&key2=value2`, and neither does it test for it. Wget will simply

transmit whatever data is provided to it. Most servers however expect the POST data to be in the above format when processing HTML Forms.

Please be aware that Wget needs to know the size of the POST data in advance. Therefore the argument to `--post-file` must be a regular file; specifying a FIFO or something like `/dev/stdin` won't work. It's not quite clear how to work around this limitation inherent in HTTP/1.0. Although HTTP/1.1 introduces *chunked* transfer that doesn't require knowing the request length in advance, a client can't use chunked unless it knows it's talking to an HTTP/1.1 server. And it can't know that until it receives a response, which in turn requires the request to have been completed – a chicken-and-egg problem.

Note: As of version 1.15 if Wget is redirected after the POST request is completed, its behaviour will depend on the response code returned by the server. In case of a 301 Moved Permanently, 302 Moved Temporarily or 307 Temporary Redirect, Wget will, in accordance with RFC2616, continue to send a POST request. In case a server wants the client to change the Request method upon redirection, it should send a 303 See Other response code.

This example shows how to log in to a server using POST and then proceed to download the desired pages, presumably only accessible to authorized users:

```
# Log in to the server.  This can be done only once.
wget --save-cookies cookies.txt \
     --post-data 'user=foo&password=bar' \
     http://server.com/auth.php


# Now grab the page or pages we care about.
wget --load-cookies cookies.txt \
     -p http://server.com/interesting/article.php
```

If the server is using session cookies to track user authentication, the above will not work because '`--save-cookies`' will not save them (and neither will browsers) and the `cookies.txt` file will be empty. In that case use '`--keep-session-cookies`' along with '`--save-cookies`' to force saving of session cookies.

'`--method=HTTP-Method`'

> For the purpose of RESTful scripting, Wget allows sending of other HTTP Methods without the need to explicitly set them using '`--header=Header-Line`'. Wget will use whatever string is passed to it after '`--method`' as the HTTP Method to the server.

'`--body-data=Data-String`'
'`--body-file=Data-File`'

> Must be set when additional data needs to be sent to the server along with the Method specified using '`--method`'. '`--body-data`' sends *string* as data, whereas '`--body-file`' sends the contents of *file*. Other than that, they work in exactly the same way.
>
> Currently, '`--body-file`' is *not* for transmitting files as a whole. Wget does not currently support `multipart/form-data` for transmitting data; only `application/x-www-form-urlencoded`. In the future, this may be changed so that wget sends the '`--body-file`' as a complete file instead of sending its contents to the server. Please be aware that Wget needs to know the contents of BODY Data in advance, and hence the argument to '`--body-file`' should be a regular file. See '`--post-file`' for a more detailed explanation. Only one of '`--body-data`' and '`--body-file`' should be specified.

If Wget is redirected after the request is completed, Wget will suspend the current method and send a GET request till the redirection is completed. This is true for all redirection response codes except 307 Temporary Redirect which is used to explicitly specify that the request method should *not* change. Another exception is when the method is set to POST, in which case the redirection rules specified under '--post-data' are followed.

'--content-disposition'

If this is set to on, experimental (not fully-functional) support for Content-Disposition headers is enabled. This can currently result in extra round-trips to the server for a HEAD request, and is known to suffer from a few bugs, which is why it is not currently enabled by default.

This option is useful for some file-downloading CGI programs that use Content-Disposition headers to describe what the name of a downloaded file should be.

'--content-on-error'

If this is set to on, wget will not skip the content when the server responds with a http status code that indicates error.

'--trust-server-names'

If this is set to on, on a redirect the last component of the redirection URL will be used as the local file name. By default it is used the last component in the original URL.

'--auth-no-challenge'

If this option is given, Wget will send Basic HTTP authentication information (plaintext username and password) for all requests, just like Wget 1.10.2 and prior did by default.

Use of this option is not recommended, and is intended only to support some few obscure servers, which never send HTTP authentication challenges, but accept unsolicited auth info, say, in addition to form-based authentication.

2.8 HTTPS (SSL/TLS) Options

To support encrypted HTTP (HTTPS) downloads, Wget must be compiled with an external SSL library, currently OpenSSL. If Wget is compiled without SSL support, none of these options are available.

'--secure-protocol=*protocol*'

Choose the secure protocol to be used. Legal values are 'auto', 'SSLv2', 'SSLv3', 'TLSv1', 'TLSv1_1', 'TLSv1_2' and 'PFS'. If 'auto' is used, the SSL library is given the liberty of choosing the appropriate protocol automatically, which is achieved by sending a TLSv1 greeting. This is the default.

Specifying 'SSLv2', 'SSLv3', 'TLSv1', 'TLSv1_1' or 'TLSv1_2' forces the use of the corresponding protocol. This is useful when talking to old and buggy SSL server implementations that make it hard for the underlying SSL library to choose the correct protocol version. Fortunately, such servers are quite rare.

Specifying 'PFS' enforces the use of the so-called Perfect Forward Security cipher suites. In short, PFS adds security by creating a one-time key for each SSL connection. It has a bit more CPU impact on client and server. We use known to be secure ciphers (e.g. no MD4) and the TLS protocol.

'--https-only'

When in recursive mode, only HTTPS links are followed.

'`--no-check-certificate`'

> Don't check the server certificate against the available certificate authorities. Also don't require the URL host name to match the common name presented by the certificate.
>
> As of Wget 1.10, the default is to verify the server's certificate against the recognized certificate authorities, breaking the SSL handshake and aborting the download if the verification fails. Although this provides more secure downloads, it does break interoperability with some sites that worked with previous Wget versions, particularly those using self-signed, expired, or otherwise invalid certificates. This option forces an "insecure" mode of operation that turns the certificate verification errors into warnings and allows you to proceed.
>
> If you encounter "certificate verification" errors or ones saying that "common name doesn't match requested host name", you can use this option to bypass the verification and proceed with the download. *Only use this option if you are otherwise convinced of the site's authenticity, or if you really don't care about the validity of its certificate.* It is almost always a bad idea not to check the certificates when transmitting confidential or important data.

'`--certificate=file`'

> Use the client certificate stored in *file*. This is needed for servers that are configured to require certificates from the clients that connect to them. Normally a certificate is not required and this switch is optional.

'`--certificate-type=type`'

> Specify the type of the client certificate. Legal values are '`PEM`' (assumed by default) and '`DER`', also known as '`ASN1`'.

'`--private-key=file`'

> Read the private key from *file*. This allows you to provide the private key in a file separate from the certificate.

'`--private-key-type=type`'

> Specify the type of the private key. Accepted values are '`PEM`' (the default) and '`DER`'.

'`--ca-certificate=file`'

> Use *file* as the file with the bundle of certificate authorities ("CA") to verify the peers. The certificates must be in PEM format.
>
> Without this option Wget looks for CA certificates at the system-specified locations, chosen at OpenSSL installation time.

'`--ca-directory=directory`'

> Specifies directory containing CA certificates in PEM format. Each file contains one CA certificate, and the file name is based on a hash value derived from the certificate. This is achieved by processing a certificate directory with the `c_rehash` utility supplied with OpenSSL. Using '`--ca-directory`' is more efficient than '`--ca-certificate`' when many certificates are installed because it allows Wget to fetch certificates on demand.
>
> Without this option Wget looks for CA certificates at the system-specified locations, chosen at OpenSSL installation time.

'`--crl-file=file`'

> Specifies a CRL file in *file*. This is needed for certificates that have been revoked by the CAs.

'`--random-file=file`'

> [OpenSSL and LibreSSL only] Use *file* as the source of random data for seeding the pseudo-random number generator on systems without `/dev/urandom`.
>
> On such systems the SSL library needs an external source of randomness to initialize. Randomness may be provided by EGD (see '`--egd-file`' below) or read from an external source specified by the user. If this option is not specified, Wget looks for random data in `$RANDFILE` or, if that is unset, in `$HOME/.rnd`.
>
> If you're getting the "Could not seed OpenSSL PRNG; disabling SSL." error, you should provide random data using some of the methods described above.

'`--egd-file=file`'

> [OpenSSL only] Use *file* as the EGD socket. EGD stands for *Entropy Gathering Daemon*, a user-space program that collects data from various unpredictable system sources and makes it available to other programs that might need it. Encryption software, such as the SSL library, needs sources of non-repeating randomness to seed the random number generator used to produce cryptographically strong keys.
>
> OpenSSL allows the user to specify his own source of entropy using the `RAND_FILE` environment variable. If this variable is unset, or if the specified file does not produce enough randomness, OpenSSL will read random data from EGD socket specified using this option.
>
> If this option is not specified (and the equivalent startup command is not used), EGD is never contacted. EGD is not needed on modern Unix systems that support `/dev/urandom`.

'`--warc-file=file`'

> Use *file* as the destination WARC file.

'`--warc-header=string`'

> Use *string* into as the warcinfo record.

'`--warc-max-size=size`'

> Set the maximum size of the WARC files to *size*.

'`--warc-cdx`'

> Write CDX index files.

'`--warc-dedup=file`'

> Do not store records listed in this CDX file.

'`--no-warc-compression`'

> Do not compress WARC files with GZIP.

'`--no-warc-digests`'

> Do not calculate SHA1 digests.

'`--no-warc-keep-log`'

> Do not store the log file in a WARC record.

'`--warc-tempdir=dir`'

> Specify the location for temporary files created by the WARC writer.

2.9 FTP Options

'`--ftp-user=user`'
'`--ftp-password=password`'

> Specify the username *user* and password *password* on an FTP server. Without this, or the corresponding startup option, the password defaults to '`-wget@`', normally used for anonymous FTP.

Another way to specify username and password is in the URL itself (see Section 2.1 [URL Format], page 2). Either method reveals your password to anyone who bothers to run ps. To prevent the passwords from being seen, store them in .wgetrc or .netrc, and make sure to protect those files from other users with chmod. If the passwords are really important, do not leave them lying in those files either—edit the files and delete them after Wget has started the download.

See Section 9.2 [Security Considerations], page 54, for more information about security issues with Wget.

'--no-remove-listing'

Don't remove the temporary .listing files generated by FTP retrievals. Normally, these files contain the raw directory listings received from FTP servers. Not removing them can be useful for debugging purposes, or when you want to be able to easily check on the contents of remote server directories (e.g. to verify that a mirror you're running is complete).

Note that even though Wget writes to a known filename for this file, this is not a security hole in the scenario of a user making .listing a symbolic link to /etc/passwd or something and asking root to run Wget in his or her directory. Depending on the options used, either Wget will refuse to write to .listing, making the globbing/recursion/time-stamping operation fail, or the symbolic link will be deleted and replaced with the actual .listing file, or the listing will be written to a .listing.number file.

Even though this situation isn't a problem, though, root should never run Wget in a non-trusted user's directory. A user could do something as simple as linking index.html to /etc/passwd and asking root to run Wget with '-N' or '-r' so the file will be overwritten.

'--no-glob'

Turn off FTP globbing. Globbing refers to the use of shell-like special characters (*wildcards*), like '*', '?', '[' and ']' to retrieve more than one file from the same directory at once, like:

    wget ftp://gnjilux.srk.fer.hr/*.msg

By default, globbing will be turned on if the URL contains a globbing character. This option may be used to turn globbing on or off permanently.

You may have to quote the URL to protect it from being expanded by your shell. Globbing makes Wget look for a directory listing, which is system-specific. This is why it currently works only with Unix FTP servers (and the ones emulating Unix ls output).

'--no-passive-ftp'

Disable the use of the *passive* FTP transfer mode. Passive FTP mandates that the client connect to the server to establish the data connection rather than the other way around.

If the machine is connected to the Internet directly, both passive and active FTP should work equally well. Behind most firewall and NAT configurations passive FTP has a better chance of working. However, in some rare firewall configurations, active FTP actually works when passive FTP doesn't. If you suspect this to be the case, use this option, or set passive_ftp=off in your init file.

'--preserve-permissions'

Preserve remote file permissions instead of permissions set by umask.

'--retr-symlinks'

> By default, when retrieving FTP directories recursively and a symbolic link is encoun-
> tered, the symbolic link is traversed and the pointed-to files are retrieved. Currently,
> Wget does not traverse symbolic links to directories to download them recursively,
> though this feature may be added in the future.
>
> When '--retr-symlinks=no' is specified, the linked-to file is not downloaded. In-
> stead, a matching symbolic link is created on the local filesystem. The pointed-to
> file will not be retrieved unless this recursive retrieval would have encountered it
> separately and downloaded it anyway. This option poses a security risk where a
> malicious FTP Server may cause Wget to write to files outside of the intended
> directories through a specially crafted .LISTING file.
>
> Note that when retrieving a file (not a directory) because it was specified on the
> command-line, rather than because it was recursed to, this option has no effect.
> Symbolic links are always traversed in this case.

2.10 Recursive Retrieval Options

'-r'
'--recursive'

> Turn on recursive retrieving. See Chapter 3 [Recursive Download], page 28, for more
> details. The default maximum depth is 5.

'-l depth'
'--level=depth'

> Specify recursion maximum depth level depth (see Chapter 3 [Recursive Download],
> page 28).

'--delete-after'

> This option tells Wget to delete every single file it downloads, *after* having done so.
> It is useful for pre-fetching popular pages through a proxy, e.g.:
>
>   wget -r -nd --delete-after http://whatever.com/~popular/page/
>
> The '-r' option is to retrieve recursively, and '-nd' to not create directories.
>
> Note that '--delete-after' deletes files on the local machine. It does not is-
> sue the 'DELE' command to remote FTP sites, for instance. Also note that when
> '--delete-after' is specified, '--convert-links' is ignored, so '.orig' files are
> simply not created in the first place.

'-k'
'--convert-links'

> After the download is complete, convert the links in the document to make them
> suitable for local viewing. This affects not only the visible hyperlinks, but any part
> of the document that links to external content, such as embedded images, links to
> style sheets, hyperlinks to non-HTML content, etc.
>
> Each link will be changed in one of the two ways:
>
> - The links to files that have been downloaded by Wget will be changed to refer
>   to the file they point to as a relative link.
>
>   Example: if the downloaded file /foo/doc.html links to /bar/img.gif,
>   also downloaded, then the link in doc.html will be modified to point to
>   '../bar/img.gif'. This kind of transformation works reliably for arbitrary
>   combinations of directories.
>
> - The links to files that have not been downloaded by Wget will be changed to
>   include host name and absolute path of the location they point to.

Example: if the downloaded file `/foo/doc.html` links to `/bar/img.gif` (or to `../bar/img.gif`), then the link in `doc.html` will be modified to point to `http://hostname/bar/img.gif`.

Because of this, local browsing works reliably: if a linked file was downloaded, the link will refer to its local name; if it was not downloaded, the link will refer to its full Internet address rather than presenting a broken link. The fact that the former links are converted to relative links ensures that you can move the downloaded hierarchy to another directory.

Note that only at the end of the download can Wget know which links have been downloaded. Because of that, the work done by '-k' will be performed at the end of all the downloads.

'-K'

'--backup-converted'

When converting a file, back up the original version with a '.orig' suffix. Affects the behavior of '-N' (see Section 5.2 [HTTP Time-Stamping Internals], page 34).

'-m'

'--mirror'

Turn on options suitable for mirroring. This option turns on recursion and time-stamping, sets infinite recursion depth and keeps FTP directory listings. It is currently equivalent to '-r -N -l inf --no-remove-listing'.

'-p'

'--page-requisites'

This option causes Wget to download all the files that are necessary to properly display a given HTML page. This includes such things as inlined images, sounds, and referenced stylesheets.

Ordinarily, when downloading a single HTML page, any requisite documents that may be needed to display it properly are not downloaded. Using '-r' together with '-l' can help, but since Wget does not ordinarily distinguish between external and inlined documents, one is generally left with "leaf documents" that are missing their requisites.

For instance, say document `1.html` contains an `<IMG>` tag referencing `1.gif` and an `<A>` tag pointing to external document `2.html`. Say that `2.html` is similar but that its image is `2.gif` and it links to `3.html`. Say this continues up to some arbitrarily high number.

If one executes the command:

    wget -r -l 2 http://site/1.html

then `1.html`, `1.gif`, `2.html`, `2.gif`, and `3.html` will be downloaded. As you can see, `3.html` is without its requisite `3.gif` because Wget is simply counting the number of hops (up to 2) away from `1.html` in order to determine where to stop the recursion. However, with this command:

    wget -r -l 2 -p http://site/1.html

all the above files *and* `3.html`'s requisite `3.gif` will be downloaded. Similarly,

    wget -r -l 1 -p http://site/1.html

will cause `1.html`, `1.gif`, `2.html`, and `2.gif` to be downloaded. One might think that:

    wget -r -l 0 -p http://site/1.html

would download just `1.html` and `1.gif`, but unfortunately this is not the case, because '-l 0' is equivalent to '-l inf'—that is, infinite recursion. To download a single HTML page (or a handful of them, all specified on the command-line or in a '-i' URL input file) and its (or their) requisites, simply leave off '-r' and '-l':

        wget -p http://*site*/1.html

Note that Wget will behave as if '-r' had been specified, but only that single page and its requisites will be downloaded. Links from that page to external documents will not be followed. Actually, to download a single page and all its requisites (even if they exist on separate websites), and make sure the lot displays properly locally, this author likes to use a few options in addition to '-p':

        wget -E -H -k -K -p http://*site*/*document*

To finish off this topic, it's worth knowing that Wget's idea of an external document link is any URL specified in an <A> tag, an <AREA> tag, or a <LINK> tag other than <LINK REL="stylesheet">.

'--strict-comments'

> Turn on strict parsing of HTML comments. The default is to terminate comments at the first occurrence of '-->'.
>
> According to specifications, HTML comments are expressed as SGML *declarations*. Declaration is special markup that begins with '<!' and ends with '>', such as '<!DOCTYPE ...>', that may contain comments between a pair of '--' delimiters. HTML comments are "empty declarations", SGML declarations without any non-comment text. Therefore, '<!--foo-->' is a valid comment, and so is '<!--one----two-->', but '<!--1--2-->' is not.
>
> On the other hand, most HTML writers don't perceive comments as anything other than text delimited with '<!--' and '-->', which is not quite the same. For example, something like '<!----------->' works as a valid comment as long as the number of dashes is a multiple of four (!). If not, the comment technically lasts until the next '--', which may be at the other end of the document. Because of this, many popular browsers completely ignore the specification and implement what users have come to expect: comments delimited with '<!--' and '-->'.
>
> Until version 1.9, Wget interpreted comments strictly, which resulted in missing links in many web pages that displayed fine in browsers, but had the misfortune of containing non-compliant comments. Beginning with version 1.9, Wget has joined the ranks of clients that implements "naive" comments, terminating each comment at the first occurrence of '-->'.
>
> If, for whatever reason, you want strict comment parsing, use this option to turn it on.

2.11 Recursive Accept/Reject Options

'-A *acclist* --accept *acclist*'
'-R *rejlist* --reject *rejlist*'

> Specify comma-separated lists of file name suffixes or patterns to accept or reject (see Section 4.2 [Types of Files], page 29). Note that if any of the wildcard characters, '*', '?', '[' or ']', appear in an element of *acclist* or *rejlist*, it will be treated as a pattern, rather than a suffix. In this case, you have to enclose the pattern into quotes to prevent your shell from expanding it, like in '-A "*.mp3"' or '-A '*.mp3''.

'--accept-regex *urlregex*'
'--reject-regex *urlregex*'

> Specify a regular expression to accept or reject the complete URL.

'--regex-type *regextype*'

>Specify the regular expression type. Possible types are 'posix' or 'pcre'. Note that to be able to use 'pcre' type, wget has to be compiled with libpcre support.

'-D *domain-list*'
'--domains=*domain-list*'

>Set domains to be followed. *domain-list* is a comma-separated list of domains. Note that it does *not* turn on '-H'.

'--exclude-domains *domain-list*'

>Specify the domains that are *not* to be followed (see Section 4.1 [Spanning Hosts], page 29).

'--follow-ftp'

>Follow FTP links from HTML documents. Without this option, Wget will ignore all the FTP links.

'--follow-tags=*list*'

>Wget has an internal table of HTML tag / attribute pairs that it considers when looking for linked documents during a recursive retrieval. If a user wants only a subset of those tags to be considered, however, he or she should be specify such tags in a comma-separated *list* with this option.

'--ignore-tags=*list*'

>This is the opposite of the '--follow-tags' option. To skip certain HTML tags when recursively looking for documents to download, specify them in a comma-separated *list*.

>In the past, this option was the best bet for downloading a single page and its requisites, using a command-line like:

>>wget --ignore-tags=a,area -H -k -K -r http://*site/document*

>However, the author of this option came across a page with tags like <LINK REL="home" HREF="/"> and came to the realization that specifying tags to ignore was not enough. One can't just tell Wget to ignore <LINK>, because then stylesheets will not be downloaded. Now the best bet for downloading a single page and its requisites is the dedicated '--page-requisites' option.

'--ignore-case'

>Ignore case when matching files and directories. This influences the behavior of -R, -A, -I, and -X options, as well as globbing implemented when downloading from FTP sites. For example, with this option, '-A "*.txt"' will match 'file1.txt', but also 'file2.TXT', 'file3.TxT', and so on. The quotes in the example are to prevent the shell from expanding the pattern.

'-H'
'--span-hosts'

>Enable spanning across hosts when doing recursive retrieving (see Section 4.1 [Spanning Hosts], page 29).

'-L'
'--relative'

>Follow relative links only. Useful for retrieving a specific home page without any distractions, not even those from the same hosts (see Section 4.4 [Relative Links], page 32).

'-I *list*'
'--include-directories=*list*'

> Specify a comma-separated list of directories you wish to follow when downloading (see Section 4.3 [Directory-Based Limits], page 31). Elements of *list* may contain wildcards.

'-X *list*'
'--exclude-directories=*list*'

> Specify a comma-separated list of directories you wish to exclude from download (see Section 4.3 [Directory-Based Limits], page 31). Elements of *list* may contain wildcards.

'-np'

'--no-parent'

> Do not ever ascend to the parent directory when retrieving recursively. This is a useful option, since it guarantees that only the files *below* a certain hierarchy will be downloaded. See Section 4.3 [Directory-Based Limits], page 31, for more details.

2.12 Exit Status

Wget may return one of several error codes if it encounters problems.

0	No problems occurred.
1	Generic error code.
2	Parse error—for instance, when parsing command-line options, the '.wgetrc' or '.netrc'...
3	File I/O error.
4	Network failure.
5	SSL verification failure.
6	Username/password authentication failure.
7	Protocol errors.
8	Server issued an error response.

With the exceptions of 0 and 1, the lower-numbered exit codes take precedence over higher-numbered ones, when multiple types of errors are encountered.

In versions of Wget prior to 1.12, Wget's exit status tended to be unhelpful and inconsistent. Recursive downloads would virtually always return 0 (success), regardless of any issues encountered, and non-recursive fetches only returned the status corresponding to the most recently-attempted download.

3 Recursive Download

GNU Wget is capable of traversing parts of the Web (or a single HTTP or FTP server), following links and directory structure. We refer to this as to *recursive retrieval*, or *recursion*.

With HTTP URLs, Wget retrieves and parses the HTML or CSS from the given URL, retrieving the files the document refers to, through markup like `href` or `src`, or CSS URI values specified using the 'url()' functional notation. If the freshly downloaded file is also of type `text/html`, `application/xhtml+xml`, or `text/css`, it will be parsed and followed further.

Recursive retrieval of HTTP and HTML/CSS content is *breadth-first*. This means that Wget first downloads the requested document, then the documents linked from that document, then the documents linked by them, and so on. In other words, Wget first downloads the documents at depth 1, then those at depth 2, and so on until the specified maximum depth.

The maximum *depth* to which the retrieval may descend is specified with the '-1' option. The default maximum depth is five layers.

When retrieving an FTP URL recursively, Wget will retrieve all the data from the given directory tree (including the subdirectories up to the specified depth) on the remote server, creating its mirror image locally. FTP retrieval is also limited by the `depth` parameter. Unlike HTTP recursion, FTP recursion is performed depth-first.

By default, Wget will create a local directory tree, corresponding to the one found on the remote server.

Recursive retrieving can find a number of applications, the most important of which is mirroring. It is also useful for WWW presentations, and any other opportunities where slow network connections should be bypassed by storing the files locally.

You should be warned that recursive downloads can overload the remote servers. Because of that, many administrators frown upon them and may ban access from your site if they detect very fast downloads of big amounts of content. When downloading from Internet servers, consider using the '-w' option to introduce a delay between accesses to the server. The download will take a while longer, but the server administrator will not be alarmed by your rudeness.

Of course, recursive download may cause problems on your machine. If left to run unchecked, it can easily fill up the disk. If downloading from local network, it can also take bandwidth on the system, as well as consume memory and CPU.

Try to specify the criteria that match the kind of download you are trying to achieve. If you want to download only one page, use '--page-requisites' without any additional recursion. If you want to download things under one directory, use '-np' to avoid downloading things from other directories. If you want to download all the files from one directory, use '-1 1' to make sure the recursion depth never exceeds one. See Chapter 4 [Following Links], page 29, for more information about this.

Recursive retrieval should be used with care. Don't say you were not warned.

4 Following Links

When retrieving recursively, one does not wish to retrieve loads of unnecessary data. Most of the time the users bear in mind exactly what they want to download, and want Wget to follow only specific links.

For example, if you wish to download the music archive from 'fly.srk.fer.hr', you will not want to download all the home pages that happen to be referenced by an obscure part of the archive.

Wget possesses several mechanisms that allows you to fine-tune which links it will follow.

4.1 Spanning Hosts

Wget's recursive retrieval normally refuses to visit hosts different than the one you specified on the command line. This is a reasonable default; without it, every retrieval would have the potential to turn your Wget into a small version of google.

However, visiting different hosts, or *host spanning*, is sometimes a useful option. Maybe the images are served from a different server. Maybe you're mirroring a site that consists of pages interlinked between three servers. Maybe the server has two equivalent names, and the HTML pages refer to both interchangeably.

Span to any host—'-H'
> The '-H' option turns on host spanning, thus allowing Wget's recursive run to visit any host referenced by a link. Unless sufficient recursion-limiting criteria are applied depth, these foreign hosts will typically link to yet more hosts, and so on until Wget ends up sucking up much more data than you have intended.

Limit spanning to certain domains—'-D'
> The '-D' option allows you to specify the domains that will be followed, thus limiting the recursion only to the hosts that belong to these domains. Obviously, this makes sense only in conjunction with '-H'. A typical example would be downloading the contents of 'www.server.com', but allowing downloads from 'images.server.com', etc.:
>
>   wget -rH -Dserver.com http://www.server.com/
>
> You can specify more than one address by separating them with a comma, e.g. '-Ddomain1.com,domain2.com'.

Keep download off certain domains—'--exclude-domains'
> If there are domains you want to exclude specifically, you can do it with '--exclude-domains', which accepts the same type of arguments of '-D', but will *exclude* all the listed domains. For example, if you want to download all the hosts from 'foo.edu' domain, with the exception of 'sunsite.foo.edu', you can do it like this:
>
>   wget -rH -Dfoo.edu --exclude-domains sunsite.foo.edu \
>   http://www.foo.edu/

4.2 Types of Files

When downloading material from the web, you will often want to restrict the retrieval to only certain file types. For example, if you are interested in downloading GIFs, you will not be overjoyed to get loads of PostScript documents, and vice versa.

Wget offers two options to deal with this problem. Each option description lists a short name, a long name, and the equivalent command in .wgetrc.

'-A *acclist*'
'--accept *acclist*'
'accept = *acclist*'
'--accept-regex *urlregex*'
'accept-regex = *urlregex*'

> The argument to '--accept' option is a list of file suffixes or patterns that Wget will download during recursive retrieval. A suffix is the ending part of a file, and consists of "normal" letters, e.g. 'gif' or '.jpg'. A matching pattern contains shell-like wildcards, e.g. 'books*' or 'zelazny*196[0-9]*'.

> So, specifying 'wget -A gif,jpg' will make Wget download only the files ending with 'gif' or 'jpg', i.e. GIFs and JPEGs. On the other hand, 'wget -A "zelazny*196[0-9]*"' will download only files beginning with 'zelazny' and containing numbers from 1960 to 1969 anywhere within. Look up the manual of your shell for a description of how pattern matching works.

> Of course, any number of suffixes and patterns can be combined into a comma-separated list, and given as an argument to '-A'.

> The argument to '--accept-regex' option is a regular expression which is matched against the complete URL.

'-R *rejlist*'
'--reject *rejlist*'
'reject = *rejlist*'
'--reject-regex *urlregex*'
'reject-regex = *urlregex*'

> The '--reject' option works the same way as '--accept', only its logic is the reverse; Wget will download all files *except* the ones matching the suffixes (or patterns) in the list.

> So, if you want to download a whole page except for the cumbersome MPEGs and .AU files, you can use 'wget -R mpg,mpeg,au'. Analogously, to download all files except the ones beginning with 'bjork', use 'wget -R "bjork*"'. The quotes are to prevent expansion by the shell.

The argument to '--accept-regex' option is a regular expression which is matched against the complete URL.

The '-A' and '-R' options may be combined to achieve even better fine-tuning of which files to retrieve. E.g. 'wget -A "*zelazny*" -R .ps' will download all the files having 'zelazny' as a part of their name, but *not* the PostScript files.

Note that these two options do not affect the downloading of HTML files (as determined by a '.htm' or '.html' filename prefix). This behavior may not be desirable for all users, and may be changed for future versions of Wget.

Note, too, that query strings (strings at the end of a URL beginning with a question mark ('?') are not included as part of the filename for accept/reject rules, even though these will actually contribute to the name chosen for the local file. It is expected that a future version of Wget will provide an option to allow matching against query strings.

Finally, it's worth noting that the accept/reject lists are matched *twice* against downloaded files: once against the URL's filename portion, to determine if the file should be downloaded in the first place; then, after it has been accepted and successfully downloaded, the local file's name is also checked against the accept/reject lists to see if it should be removed. The rationale was that, since '.htm' and '.html' files are always downloaded regardless of accept/reject rules, they should be removed *after* being downloaded and scanned for links, if they did match the accept/reject lists. However, this can lead to unexpected results, since the local filenames can differ from the original URL filenames in the following ways, all of which can change whether an accept/reject rule matches:

- If the local file already exists and '--no-directories' was specified, a numeric suffix will be appended to the original name.

- If '--adjust-extension' was specified, the local filename might have '.html' appended to it. If Wget is invoked with '-E -A.php', a filename such as 'index.php' will match be accepted, but upon download will be named 'index.php.html', which no longer matches, and so the file will be deleted.

- Query strings do not contribute to URL matching, but are included in local filenames, and so *do* contribute to filename matching.

This behavior, too, is considered less-than-desirable, and may change in a future version of Wget.

4.3 Directory-Based Limits

Regardless of other link-following facilities, it is often useful to place the restriction of what files to retrieve based on the directories those files are placed in. There can be many reasons for this—the home pages may be organized in a reasonable directory structure; or some directories may contain useless information, e.g. /cgi-bin or /dev directories.

Wget offers three different options to deal with this requirement. Each option description lists a short name, a long name, and the equivalent command in .wgetrc.

'-I *list*'
'--include *list*'
'include_directories = *list*'

> '-I' option accepts a comma-separated list of directories included in the retrieval. Any other directories will simply be ignored. The directories are absolute paths.
>
> So, if you wish to download from 'http://host/people/bozo/' following only links to bozo's colleagues in the /people directory and the bogus scripts in /cgi-bin, you can specify:
>
>> wget -I /people,/cgi-bin http://host/people/bozo/

'-X *list*'
'--exclude *list*'
'exclude_directories = *list*'

> '-X' option is exactly the reverse of '-I'—this is a list of directories *excluded* from the download. E.g. if you do not want Wget to download things from /cgi-bin directory, specify '-X /cgi-bin' on the command line.
>
> The same as with '-A'/'-R', these two options can be combined to get a better fine-tuning of downloading subdirectories. E.g. if you want to load all the files from /pub hierarchy except for /pub/worthless, specify '-I/pub -X/pub/worthless'.

'-np'
'--no-parent'
'no_parent = on'

> The simplest, and often very useful way of limiting directories is disallowing retrieval of the links that refer to the hierarchy *above* than the beginning directory, i.e. disallowing ascent to the parent directory/directories.
>
> The '--no-parent' option (short '-np') is useful in this case. Using it guarantees that you will never leave the existing hierarchy. Supposing you issue Wget with:
>
>> wget -r --no-parent http://somehost/~luzer/my-archive/

You may rest assured that none of the references to /~his-girls-homepage/ or /~luzer/all-my-mpegs/ will be followed. Only the archive you are interested in will be downloaded. Essentially, '--no-parent' is similar to '-I/~luzer/my-archive', only it handles redirections in a more intelligent fashion.

Note that, for HTTP (and HTTPS), the trailing slash is very important to '--no-parent'. HTTP has no concept of a "directory"—Wget relies on you to indicate what's a directory and what isn't. In 'http://foo/bar/', Wget will consider 'bar' to be a directory, while in 'http://foo/bar' (no trailing slash), 'bar' will be considered a filename (so '--no-parent' would be meaningless, as its parent is '/').

4.4 Relative Links

When '-L' is turned on, only the relative links are ever followed. Relative links are here defined those that do not refer to the web server root. For example, these links are relative:

```
<a href="foo.gif">
<a href="foo/bar.gif">
<a href="../foo/bar.gif">
```

These links are not relative:

```
<a href="/foo.gif">
<a href="/foo/bar.gif">
<a href="http://www.server.com/foo/bar.gif">
```

Using this option guarantees that recursive retrieval will not span hosts, even without '-H'. In simple cases it also allows downloads to "just work" without having to convert links.

This option is probably not very useful and might be removed in a future release.

4.5 Following FTP Links

The rules for FTP are somewhat specific, as it is necessary for them to be. FTP links in HTML documents are often included for purposes of reference, and it is often inconvenient to download them by default.

To have FTP links followed from HTML documents, you need to specify the '--follow-ftp' option. Having done that, FTP links will span hosts regardless of '-H' setting. This is logical, as FTP links rarely point to the same host where the HTTP server resides. For similar reasons, the '-L' options has no effect on such downloads. On the other hand, domain acceptance ('-D') and suffix rules ('-A' and '-R') apply normally.

Also note that followed links to FTP directories will not be retrieved recursively further.

5 Time-Stamping

One of the most important aspects of mirroring information from the Internet is updating your archives.

Downloading the whole archive again and again, just to replace a few changed files is expensive, both in terms of wasted bandwidth and money, and the time to do the update. This is why all the mirroring tools offer the option of incremental updating.

Such an updating mechanism means that the remote server is scanned in search of *new* files. Only those new files will be downloaded in the place of the old ones.

A file is considered new if one of these two conditions are met:

1. A file of that name does not already exist locally.

2. A file of that name does exist, but the remote file was modified more recently than the local file.

To implement this, the program needs to be aware of the time of last modification of both local and remote files. We call this information the *time-stamp* of a file.

The time-stamping in GNU Wget is turned on using '--timestamping' ('-N') option, or through `timestamping = on` directive in `.wgetrc`. With this option, for each file it intends to download, Wget will check whether a local file of the same name exists. If it does, and the remote file is not newer, Wget will not download it.

If the local file does not exist, or the sizes of the files do not match, Wget will download the remote file no matter what the time-stamps say.

5.1 Time-Stamping Usage

The usage of time-stamping is simple. Say you would like to download a file so that it keeps its date of modification.

    wget -S http://www.gnu.ai.mit.edu/

A simple `ls -l` shows that the time stamp on the local file equals the state of the `Last-Modified` header, as returned by the server. As you can see, the time-stamping info is preserved locally, even without '-N' (at least for HTTP).

Several days later, you would like Wget to check if the remote file has changed, and download it if it has.

    wget -N http://www.gnu.ai.mit.edu/

Wget will ask the server for the last-modified date. If the local file has the same timestamp as the server, or a newer one, the remote file will not be re-fetched. However, if the remote file is more recent, Wget will proceed to fetch it.

The same goes for FTP. For example:

    wget "ftp://ftp.ifi.uio.no/pub/emacs/gnus/*"

(The quotes around that URL are to prevent the shell from trying to interpret the '*'.)

After download, a local directory listing will show that the timestamps match those on the remote server. Reissuing the command with '-N' will make Wget re-fetch *only* the files that have been modified since the last download.

If you wished to mirror the GNU archive every week, you would use a command like the following, weekly:

    wget --timestamping -r ftp://ftp.gnu.org/pub/gnu/

Note that time-stamping will only work for files for which the server gives a timestamp. For HTTP, this depends on getting a `Last-Modified` header. For FTP, this depends on getting a directory listing with dates in a format that Wget can parse (see Section 5.3 [FTP Time-Stamping Internals], page 34).

5.2 HTTP Time-Stamping Internals

Time-stamping in HTTP is implemented by checking of the `Last-Modified` header. If you wish to retrieve the file `foo.html` through HTTP, Wget will check whether `foo.html` exists locally. If it doesn't, `foo.html` will be retrieved unconditionally.

If the file does exist locally, Wget will first check its local time-stamp (similar to the way `ls -l` checks it), and then send a `HEAD` request to the remote server, demanding the information on the remote file.

The `Last-Modified` header is examined to find which file was modified more recently (which makes it "newer"). If the remote file is newer, it will be downloaded; if it is older, Wget will give up.[1]

When '`--backup-converted`' ('`-K`') is specified in conjunction with '`-N`', server file '*X*' is compared to local file '*X*`.orig`', if extant, rather than being compared to local file '*X*', which will always differ if it's been converted by '`--convert-links`' ('`-k`').

Arguably, HTTP time-stamping should be implemented using the `If-Modified-Since` request.

5.3 FTP Time-Stamping Internals

In theory, FTP time-stamping works much the same as HTTP, only FTP has no headers—time-stamps must be ferreted out of directory listings.

If an FTP download is recursive or uses globbing, Wget will use the FTP `LIST` command to get a file listing for the directory containing the desired file(s). It will try to analyze the listing, treating it like Unix `ls -l` output, extracting the time-stamps. The rest is exactly the same as for HTTP. Note that when retrieving individual files from an FTP server without using globbing or recursion, listing files will not be downloaded (and thus files will not be time-stamped) unless '`-N`' is specified.

Assumption that every directory listing is a Unix-style listing may sound extremely constraining, but in practice it is not, as many non-Unix FTP servers use the Unixoid listing format because most (all?) of the clients understand it. Bear in mind that RFC959 defines no standard way to get a file list, let alone the time-stamps. We can only hope that a future standard will define this.

Another non-standard solution includes the use of `MDTM` command that is supported by some FTP servers (including the popular `wu-ftpd`), which returns the exact time of the specified file. Wget may support this command in the future.

---

[1] As an additional check, Wget will look at the `Content-Length` header, and compare the sizes; if they are not the same, the remote file will be downloaded no matter what the time-stamp says.

6 Startup File

Once you know how to change default settings of Wget through command line arguments, you may wish to make some of those settings permanent. You can do that in a convenient way by creating the Wget startup file—`.wgetrc`.

Besides `.wgetrc` is the "main" initialization file, it is convenient to have a special facility for storing passwords. Thus Wget reads and interprets the contents of `$HOME/.netrc`, if it finds it. You can find `.netrc` format in your system manuals.

Wget reads `.wgetrc` upon startup, recognizing a limited set of commands.

6.1 Wgetrc Location

When initializing, Wget will look for a *global* startup file, `/usr/local/etc/wgetrc` by default (or some prefix other than `/usr/local`, if Wget was not installed there) and read commands from there, if it exists.

Then it will look for the user's file. If the environmental variable `WGETRC` is set, Wget will try to load that file. Failing that, no further attempts will be made.

If `WGETRC` is not set, Wget will try to load `$HOME/.wgetrc`.

The fact that user's settings are loaded after the system-wide ones means that in case of collision user's wgetrc *overrides* the system-wide wgetrc (in `/usr/local/etc/wgetrc` by default). Fascist admins, away!

6.2 Wgetrc Syntax

The syntax of a wgetrc command is simple:

```
variable = value
```

The *variable* will also be called *command*. Valid *values* are different for different commands.

The commands are case-, underscore- and minus-insensitive. Thus 'DIr__PrefiX', 'DIr-PrefiX' and 'dirprefix' are the same. Empty lines, lines beginning with '#' and lines containing white-space only are discarded.

Commands that expect a comma-separated list will clear the list on an empty command. So, if you wish to reset the rejection list specified in global `wgetrc`, you can do it with:

```
reject =
```

6.3 Wgetrc Commands

The complete set of commands is listed below. Legal values are listed after the '='. Simple Boolean values can be set or unset using 'on' and 'off' or '1' and '0'.

Some commands take pseudo-arbitrary values. *address* values can be hostnames or dotted-quad IP addresses. *n* can be any positive integer, or 'inf' for infinity, where appropriate. *string* values can be any non-empty string.

Most of these commands have direct command-line equivalents. Also, any wgetrc command can be specified on the command line using the '--execute' switch (see Section 2.3 [Basic Startup Options], page 3.)

accept/reject = *string*
> Same as '-A'/'-R' (see Section 4.2 [Types of Files], page 29).

add_hostdir = on/off
> Enable/disable host-prefixed file names. '-nH' disables it.

ask_password = on/off

> Prompt for a password for each connection established. Cannot be specified when '--password' is being used, because they are mutually exclusive. Equivalent to '--ask-password'.

auth_no_challenge = on/off

> If this option is given, Wget will send Basic HTTP authentication information (plaintext username and password) for all requests. See '--auth-no-challenge'.

background = on/off

> Enable/disable going to background—the same as '-b' (which enables it).

backup_converted = on/off

> Enable/disable saving pre-converted files with the suffix '.orig'—the same as '-K' (which enables it).

backups = number

> Use up to number backups for a file. Backups are rotated by adding an incremental counter that starts at '1'. The default is '0'.

base = string

> Consider relative URLs in input files (specified via the 'input' command or the '--input-file'/'-i' option, together with 'force_html' or '--force-html') as being relative to string—the same as '--base=string'.

bind_address = address

> Bind to address, like the '--bind-address=address'.

ca_certificate = file

> Set the certificate authority bundle file to file. The same as '--ca-certificate=file'.

ca_directory = directory

> Set the directory used for certificate authorities. The same as '--ca-directory=directory'.

cache = on/off

> When set to off, disallow server-caching. See the '--no-cache' option.

certificate = file

> Set the client certificate file name to file. The same as '--certificate=file'.

certificate_type = string

> Specify the type of the client certificate, legal values being 'PEM' (the default) and 'DER' (aka ASN1). The same as '--certificate-type=string'.

check_certificate = on/off

> If this is set to off, the server certificate is not checked against the specified client authorities. The default is "on". The same as '--check-certificate'.

connect_timeout = n

> Set the connect timeout—the same as '--connect-timeout'.

content_disposition = on/off

> Turn on recognition of the (non-standard) 'Content-Disposition' HTTP header— if set to 'on', the same as '--content-disposition'.

trust_server_names = on/off

> If set to on, use the last component of a redirection URL for the local file name.

continue = on/off

> If set to on, force continuation of preexistent partially retrieved files. See '-c' before setting it.

convert_links = on/off

> Convert non-relative links locally. The same as '-k'.

cookies = on/off

> When set to off, disallow cookies. See the '--cookies' option.

cut_dirs = n

> Ignore n remote directory components. Equivalent to '--cut-dirs=n'.

debug = on/off

> Debug mode, same as '-d'.

default_page = string

> Default page name—the same as '--default-page=string'.

delete_after = on/off

> Delete after download—the same as '--delete-after'.

dir_prefix = string

> Top of directory tree—the same as '-P string'.

dirstruct = on/off

> Turning dirstruct on or off—the same as '-x' or '-nd', respectively.

dns_cache = on/off

> Turn DNS caching on/off. Since DNS caching is on by default, this option is normally used to turn it off and is equivalent to '--no-dns-cache'.

dns_timeout = n

> Set the DNS timeout—the same as '--dns-timeout'.

domains = string

> Same as '-D' (see Section 4.1 [Spanning Hosts], page 29).

dot_bytes = n

> Specify the number of bytes "contained" in a dot, as seen throughout the retrieval (1024 by default). You can postfix the value with 'k' or 'm', representing kilobytes and megabytes, respectively. With dot settings you can tailor the dot retrieval to suit your needs, or you can use the predefined *styles* (see Section 2.5 [Download Options], page 5).

dot_spacing = n

> Specify the number of dots in a single cluster (10 by default).

dots_in_line = n

> Specify the number of dots that will be printed in each line throughout the retrieval (50 by default).

egd_file = file

> Use *string* as the EGD socket file name. The same as '--egd-file=file'.

exclude_directories = string

> Specify a comma-separated list of directories you wish to exclude from download—the same as '-X string' (see Section 4.3 [Directory-Based Limits], page 31).

exclude_domains = string

> Same as '--exclude-domains=string' (see Section 4.1 [Spanning Hosts], page 29).

follow_ftp = on/off

> Follow FTP links from HTML documents—the same as '--follow-ftp'.

follow_tags = *string*

> Only follow certain HTML tags when doing a recursive retrieval, just like '--follow-tags=*string*'.

force_html = on/off

> If set to on, force the input filename to be regarded as an HTML document—the same as '-F'.

ftp_password = *string*

> Set your FTP password to *string*. Without this setting, the password defaults to '-wget@', which is a useful default for anonymous FTP access.

> This command used to be named passwd prior to Wget 1.10.

ftp_proxy = *string*

> Use *string* as FTP proxy, instead of the one specified in environment.

ftp_user = *string*

> Set FTP user to *string*.

> This command used to be named login prior to Wget 1.10.

glob = on/off

> Turn globbing on/off—the same as '--glob' and '--no-glob'.

header = *string*

> Define a header for HTTP downloads, like using '--header=*string*'.

adjust_extension = on/off

> Add a '.html' extension to 'text/html' or 'application/xhtml+xml' files that lack one, or a '.css' extension to 'text/css' files that lack one, like '-E'. Previously named 'html_extension' (still acceptable, but deprecated).

http_keep_alive = on/off

> Turn the keep-alive feature on or off (defaults to on). Turning it off is equivalent to '--no-http-keep-alive'.

http_password = *string*

> Set HTTP password, equivalent to '--http-password=*string*'.

http_proxy = *string*

> Use *string* as HTTP proxy, instead of the one specified in environment.

http_user = *string*

> Set HTTP user to *string*, equivalent to '--http-user=*string*'.

https_only = on/off

> When in recursive mode, only HTTPS links are followed (defaults to off).

https_proxy = *string*

> Use *string* as HTTPS proxy, instead of the one specified in environment.

ignore_case = on/off

> When set to on, match files and directories case insensitively; the same as '--ignore-case'.

ignore_length = on/off

> When set to on, ignore Content-Length header; the same as '--ignore-length'.

ignore_tags = *string*

> Ignore certain HTML tags when doing a recursive retrieval, like '`--ignore-tags=string`'.

include_directories = *string*

> Specify a comma-separated list of directories you wish to follow when downloading— the same as '`-I string`'.

iri = on/off

> When set to on, enable internationalized URI (IRI) support; the same as '`--iri`'.

inet4_only = on/off

> Force connecting to IPv4 addresses, off by default. You can put this in the global init file to disable Wget's attempts to resolve and connect to IPv6 hosts. Available only if Wget was compiled with IPv6 support. The same as '`--inet4-only`' or '`-4`'.

inet6_only = on/off

> Force connecting to IPv6 addresses, off by default. Available only if Wget was compiled with IPv6 support. The same as '`--inet6-only`' or '`-6`'.

input = *file*

> Read the URLs from *string*, like '`-i file`'.

keep_session_cookies = on/off

> When specified, causes '`save_cookies = on`' to also save session cookies. See '`--keep-session-cookies`'.

limit_rate = *rate*

> Limit the download speed to no more than *rate* bytes per second. The same as '`--limit-rate=rate`'.

load_cookies = *file*

> Load cookies from *file*. See '`--load-cookies file`'.

local_encoding = *encoding*

> Force Wget to use *encoding* as the default system encoding. See '`--local-encoding`'.

logfile = *file*

> Set logfile to *file*, the same as '`-o file`'.

max_redirect = *number*

> Specifies the maximum number of redirections to follow for a resource. See '`--max-redirect=number`'.

mirror = on/off

> Turn mirroring on/off. The same as '`-m`'.

netrc = on/off

> Turn reading netrc on or off.

no_clobber = on/off

> Same as '`-nc`'.

no_parent = on/off

> Disallow retrieving outside the directory hierarchy, like '`--no-parent`' (see Section 4.3 [Directory-Based Limits], page 31).

no_proxy = *string*

> Use *string* as the comma-separated list of domains to avoid in proxy loading, instead of the one specified in environment.

output_document = *file*
>   Set the output filename—the same as '-O *file*'.

page_requisites = on/off
>   Download all ancillary documents necessary for a single HTML page to display properly—the same as '-p'.

passive_ftp = on/off
>   Change setting of passive FTP, equivalent to the '--passive-ftp' option.

password = *string*
>   Specify password *string* for both FTP and HTTP file retrieval. This command can be overridden using the 'ftp_password' and 'http_password' command for FTP and HTTP respectively.

post_data = *string*
>   Use POST as the method for all HTTP requests and send *string* in the request body. The same as '--post-data=*string*'.

post_file = *file*
>   Use POST as the method for all HTTP requests and send the contents of *file* in the request body. The same as '--post-file=*file*'.

prefer_family = none/IPv4/IPv6
>   When given a choice of several addresses, connect to the addresses with specified address family first. The address order returned by DNS is used without change by default. The same as '--prefer-family', which see for a detailed discussion of why this is useful.

private_key = *file*
>   Set the private key file to *file*. The same as '--private-key=*file*'.

private_key_type = *string*
>   Specify the type of the private key, legal values being 'PEM' (the default) and 'DER' (aka ASN1). The same as '--private-type=*string*'.

progress = *string*
>   Set the type of the progress indicator. Legal types are 'dot' and 'bar'. Equivalent to '--progress=*string*'.

protocol_directories = on/off
>   When set, use the protocol name as a directory component of local file names. The same as '--protocol-directories'.

proxy_password = *string*
>   Set proxy authentication password to *string*, like '--proxy-password=*string*'.

proxy_user = *string*
>   Set proxy authentication user name to *string*, like '--proxy-user=*string*'.

quiet = on/off
>   Quiet mode—the same as '-q'.

quota = *quota*
>   Specify the download quota, which is useful to put in the global wgetrc. When download quota is specified, Wget will stop retrieving after the download sum has become greater than quota. The quota can be specified in bytes (default), kbytes ('k' appended) or mbytes ('m' appended). Thus 'quota = 5m' will set the quota to 5 megabytes. Note that the user's startup file overrides system settings.

random_file = *file*
> Use *file* as a source of randomness on systems lacking `/dev/random`.

random_wait = on/off
> Turn random between-request wait times on or off. The same as '`--random-wait`'.

read_timeout = *n*
> Set the read (and write) timeout—the same as '`--read-timeout=n`'.

reclevel = *n*
> Recursion level (depth)—the same as '`-l n`'.

recursive = on/off
> Recursive on/off—the same as '`-r`'.

referer = *string*
> Set HTTP '`Referer:`' header just like '`--referer=string`'. (Note that it was the folks who wrote the HTTP spec who got the spelling of "referrer" wrong.)

relative_only = on/off
> Follow only relative links—the same as '`-L`' (see Section 4.4 [Relative Links], page 32).

remote_encoding = *encoding*
> Force Wget to use *encoding* as the default remote server encoding. See '`--remote-encoding`'.

remove_listing = on/off
> If set to on, remove FTP listings downloaded by Wget. Setting it to off is the same as '`--no-remove-listing`'.

restrict_file_names = unix/windows
> Restrict the file names generated by Wget from URLs. See '`--restrict-file-names`' for a more detailed description.

retr_symlinks = on/off
> When set to on, retrieve symbolic links as if they were plain files; the same as '`--retr-symlinks`'.

retry_connrefused = on/off
> When set to on, consider "connection refused" a transient error—the same as '`--retry-connrefused`'.

robots = on/off
> Specify whether the norobots convention is respected by Wget, "on" by default. This switch controls both the `/robots.txt` and the '`nofollow`' aspect of the spec. See Section 9.1 [Robot Exclusion], page 53, for more details about this. Be sure you know what you are doing before turning this off.

save_cookies = *file*
> Save cookies to *file*. The same as '`--save-cookies file`'.

save_headers = on/off
> Same as '`--save-headers`'.

secure_protocol = *string*
> Choose the secure protocol to be used. Legal values are '`auto`' (the default), '`SSLv2`', '`SSLv3`', and '`TLSv1`'. The same as '`--secure-protocol=string`'.

server_response = on/off
> Choose whether or not to print the HTTP and FTP server responses—the same as '`-S`'.

show_all_dns_entries = on/off
> When a DNS name is resolved, show all the IP addresses, not just the first three.

span_hosts = on/off
> Same as '-H'.

spider = on/off
> Same as '--spider'.

strict_comments = on/off
> Same as '--strict-comments'.

timeout = n
> Set all applicable timeout values to n, the same as '-T n'.

timestamping = on/off
> Turn timestamping on/off. The same as '-N' (see Chapter 5 [Time-Stamping], page 33).

use_server_timestamps = on/off
> If set to 'off', Wget won't set the local file's timestamp by the one on the server (same as '--no-use-server-timestamps').

tries = n Set number of retries per URL—the same as '-t n'.

use_proxy = on/off
> When set to off, don't use proxy even when proxy-related environment variables are set. In that case it is the same as using '--no-proxy'.

user = *string*
> Specify username *string* for both FTP and HTTP file retrieval. This command can be overridden using the 'ftp_user' and 'http_user' command for FTP and HTTP respectively.

user_agent = *string*
> User agent identification sent to the HTTP Server—the same as '--user-agent=*string*'.

verbose = on/off
> Turn verbose on/off—the same as '-v'/'-nv'.

wait = n Wait n seconds between retrievals—the same as '-w n'.

wait_retry = n
> Wait up to n seconds between retries of failed retrievals only—the same as '--waitretry=n'. Note that this is turned on by default in the global wgetrc.

6.4 Sample Wgetrc

This is the sample initialization file, as given in the distribution. It is divided in two section—one for global usage (suitable for global startup file), and one for local usage (suitable for $HOME/.wgetrc). Be careful about the things you change.

Note that almost all the lines are commented out. For a command to have any effect, you must remove the '#' character at the beginning of its line.

```
###
### Sample Wget initialization file .wgetrc
###


## You can use this file to change the default behaviour of wget or to
```

```
## avoid having to type many many command-line options. This file does
## not contain a comprehensive list of commands -- look at the manual
## to find out what you can put into this file. You can find this here:
##    $ info wget.info 'Startup File'
## Or online here:
##    https://www.gnu.org/software/wget/manual/wget.html#Startup-File
##
## Wget initialization file can reside in /usr/local/etc/wgetrc
## (global, for all users) or $HOME/.wgetrc (for a single user).
##
## To use the settings in this file, you will have to uncomment them,
## as well as change them, in most cases, as the values on the
## commented-out lines are the default values (e.g. "off").
##
## Command are case-, underscore- and minus-insensitive.
## For example ftp_proxy, ftp-proxy and ftpproxy are the same.


##
## Global settings (useful for setting up in /usr/local/etc/wgetrc).
## Think well before you change them, since they may reduce wget's
## functionality, and make it behave contrary to the documentation:
##

# You can set retrieve quota for beginners by specifying a value
# optionally followed by 'K' (kilobytes) or 'M' (megabytes).  The
# default quota is unlimited.
#quota = inf

# You can lower (or raise) the default number of retries when
# downloading a file (default is 20).
#tries = 20

# Lowering the maximum depth of the recursive retrieval is handy to
# prevent newbies from going too "deep" when they unwittingly start
# the recursive retrieval.  The default is 5.
#reclevel = 5

# By default Wget uses "passive FTP" transfer where the client
# initiates the data connection to the server rather than the other
# way around.  That is required on systems behind NAT where the client
# computer cannot be easily reached from the Internet.  However, some
# firewalls software explicitly supports active FTP and in fact has
# problems supporting passive transfer.  If you are in such
# environment, use "passive_ftp = off" to revert to active FTP.
#passive_ftp = off

# The "wait" command below makes Wget wait between every connection.
# If, instead, you want Wget to wait only between retries of failed
# downloads, set waitretry to maximum number of seconds to wait (Wget
# will use "linear backoff", waiting 1 second after the first failure
# on a file, 2 seconds after the second failure, etc. up to this max).
```

```
#waitretry = 10


##
## Local settings (for a user to set in his $HOME/.wgetrc).  It is
## *highly* undesirable to put these settings in the global file, since
## they are potentially dangerous to "normal" users.
##
## Even when setting up your own ~/.wgetrc, you should know what you
## are doing before doing so.
##

# Set this to on to use timestamping by default:
#timestamping = off

# It is a good idea to make Wget send your email address in a 'From:'
# header with your request (so that server administrators can contact
# you in case of errors).  Wget does *not* send 'From:' by default.
#header = From: Your Name <username@site.domain>

# You can set up other headers, like Accept-Language.  Accept-Language
# is *not* sent by default.
#header = Accept-Language: en

# You can set the default proxies for Wget to use for http, https, and ftp.
# They will override the value in the environment.
#https_proxy = http://proxy.yoyodyne.com:18023/
#http_proxy = http://proxy.yoyodyne.com:18023/
#ftp_proxy = http://proxy.yoyodyne.com:18023/

# If you do not want to use proxy at all, set this to off.
#use_proxy = on

# You can customize the retrieval outlook.  Valid options are default,
# binary, mega and micro.
#dot_style = default

# Setting this to off makes Wget not download /robots.txt.  Be sure to
# know *exactly* what /robots.txt is and how it is used before changing
# the default!
#robots = on

# It can be useful to make Wget wait between connections.  Set this to
# the number of seconds you want Wget to wait.
#wait = 0

# You can force creating directory structure, even if a single is being
# retrieved, by setting this to on.
#dirstruct = off

# You can turn on recursive retrieving by default (don't do this if
# you are not sure you know what it means) by setting this to on.
```

```
#recursive = off

# To always back up file X as X.orig before converting its links (due
# to -k / --convert-links / convert_links = on having been specified),
# set this variable to on:
#backup_converted = off

# To have Wget follow FTP links from HTML files by default, set this
# to on:
#follow_ftp = off

# To try ipv6 addresses first:
#prefer-family = IPv6

# Set default IRI support state
#iri = off

# Force the default system encoding
#localencoding = UTF-8

# Force the default remote server encoding
#remoteencoding = UTF-8

# Turn on to prevent following non-HTTPS links when in recursive mode
#httpsonly = off

# Tune HTTPS security (auto, SSLv2, SSLv3, TLSv1, PFS)
#secureprotocol = auto
```

7 Examples

The examples are divided into three sections loosely based on their complexity.

7.1 Simple Usage

- Say you want to download a URL. Just type:

      wget http://fly.srk.fer.hr/

- But what will happen if the connection is slow, and the file is lengthy? The connection will probably fail before the whole file is retrieved, more than once. In this case, Wget will try getting the file until it either gets the whole of it, or exceeds the default number of retries (this being 20). It is easy to change the number of tries to 45, to insure that the whole file will arrive safely:

      wget --tries=45 http://fly.srk.fer.hr/jpg/flyweb.jpg

- Now let's leave Wget to work in the background, and write its progress to log file `log`. It is tiring to type '`--tries`', so we shall use '`-t`'.

      wget -t 45 -o log http://fly.srk.fer.hr/jpg/flyweb.jpg &

  The ampersand at the end of the line makes sure that Wget works in the background. To unlimit the number of retries, use '`-t inf`'.

- The usage of FTP is as simple. Wget will take care of login and password.

      wget ftp://gnjilux.srk.fer.hr/welcome.msg

- If you specify a directory, Wget will retrieve the directory listing, parse it and convert it to HTML. Try:

      wget ftp://ftp.gnu.org/pub/gnu/
      links index.html

7.2 Advanced Usage

- You have a file that contains the URLs you want to download? Use the '`-i`' switch:

      wget -i file

  If you specify '`-`' as file name, the URLs will be read from standard input.

- Create a five levels deep mirror image of the GNU web site, with the same directory structure the original has, with only one try per document, saving the log of the activities to `gnulog`:

      wget -r http://www.gnu.org/ -o gnulog

- The same as the above, but convert the links in the downloaded files to point to local files, so you can view the documents off-line:

      wget --convert-links -r http://www.gnu.org/ -o gnulog

- Retrieve only one HTML page, but make sure that all the elements needed for the page to be displayed, such as inline images and external style sheets, are also downloaded. Also make sure the downloaded page references the downloaded links.

      wget -p --convert-links http://www.server.com/dir/page.html

  The HTML page will be saved to `www.server.com/dir/page.html`, and the images, stylesheets, etc., somewhere under `www.server.com/`, depending on where they were on the remote server.

- The same as the above, but without the `www.server.com/` directory. In fact, I don't want to have all those random server directories anyway—just save *all* those files under a `download/` subdirectory of the current directory.

      wget -p --convert-links -nH -nd -Pdownload \
           http://www.server.com/dir/page.html

- Retrieve the index.html of 'www.lycos.com', showing the original server headers:

      wget -S http://www.lycos.com/

- Save the server headers with the file, perhaps for post-processing.

      wget --save-headers http://www.lycos.com/
      more index.html

- Retrieve the first two levels of 'wuarchive.wustl.edu', saving them to /tmp.

      wget -r -l2 -P/tmp ftp://wuarchive.wustl.edu/

- You want to download all the GIFs from a directory on an HTTP server. You tried 'wget http://www.server.com/dir/*.gif', but that didn't work because HTTP retrieval does not support globbing. In that case, use:

      wget -r -l1 --no-parent -A.gif http://www.server.com/dir/

  More verbose, but the effect is the same. '-r -l1' means to retrieve recursively (see Chapter 3 [Recursive Download], page 28), with maximum depth of 1. '--no-parent' means that references to the parent directory are ignored (see Section 4.3 [Directory-Based Limits], page 31), and '-A.gif' means to download only the GIF files. '-A "*.gif"' would have worked too.

- Suppose you were in the middle of downloading, when Wget was interrupted. Now you do not want to clobber the files already present. It would be:

      wget -nc -r http://www.gnu.org/

- If you want to encode your own username and password to HTTP or FTP, use the appropriate URL syntax (see Section 2.1 [URL Format], page 2).

      wget ftp://hniksic:mypassword@unix.server.com/.emacs

  Note, however, that this usage is not advisable on multi-user systems because it reveals your password to anyone who looks at the output of ps.

- You would like the output documents to go to standard output instead of to files?

      wget -O - http://jagor.srce.hr/ http://www.srce.hr/

  You can also combine the two options and make pipelines to retrieve the documents from remote hotlists:

      wget -O - http://cool.list.com/ | wget --force-html -i -

7.3 Very Advanced Usage

- If you wish Wget to keep a mirror of a page (or FTP subdirectories), use '--mirror' ('-m'), which is the shorthand for '-r -l inf -N'. You can put Wget in the crontab file asking it to recheck a site each Sunday:

      crontab
      0 0 * * 0 wget --mirror http://www.gnu.org/ -o /home/me/weeklog

- In addition to the above, you want the links to be converted for local viewing. But, after having read this manual, you know that link conversion doesn't play well with timestamping, so you also want Wget to back up the original HTML files before the conversion. Wget invocation would look like this:

      wget --mirror --convert-links --backup-converted \
           http://www.gnu.org/ -o /home/me/weeklog

- But you've also noticed that local viewing doesn't work all that well when HTML files are saved under extensions other than '.html', perhaps because they were served as index.cgi. So you'd like Wget to rename all the files served with content-type 'text/html' or 'application/xhtml+xml' to *name*.html.

```
wget --mirror --convert-links --backup-converted \
     --html-extension -o /home/me/weeklog          \
     http://www.gnu.org/
```

Or, with less typing:

```
wget -m -k -K -E http://www.gnu.org/ -o /home/me/weeklog
```

8 Various

This chapter contains all the stuff that could not fit anywhere else.

8.1 Proxies

Proxies are special-purpose HTTP servers designed to transfer data from remote servers to local clients. One typical use of proxies is lightening network load for users behind a slow connection. This is achieved by channeling all HTTP and FTP requests through the proxy which caches the transferred data. When a cached resource is requested again, proxy will return the data from cache. Another use for proxies is for companies that separate (for security reasons) their internal networks from the rest of Internet. In order to obtain information from the Web, their users connect and retrieve remote data using an authorized proxy.

Wget supports proxies for both HTTP and FTP retrievals. The standard way to specify proxy location, which Wget recognizes, is using the following environment variables:

```
http_proxy
https_proxy
```
> If set, the `http_proxy` and `https_proxy` variables should contain the URLs of the proxies for HTTP and HTTPS connections respectively.

```
ftp_proxy
```
> This variable should contain the URL of the proxy for FTP connections. It is quite common that `http_proxy` and `ftp_proxy` are set to the same URL.

`no_proxy` This variable should contain a comma-separated list of domain extensions proxy should *not* be used for. For instance, if the value of `no_proxy` is '`.mit.edu`', proxy will not be used to retrieve documents from MIT.

In addition to the environment variables, proxy location and settings may be specified from within Wget itself.

'`--no-proxy`'
'`proxy = on/off`'
> This option and the corresponding command may be used to suppress the use of proxy, even if the appropriate environment variables are set.

'`http_proxy = URL`'
'`https_proxy = URL`'
'`ftp_proxy = URL`'
'`no_proxy = string`'
> These startup file variables allow you to override the proxy settings specified by the environment.

Some proxy servers require authorization to enable you to use them. The authorization consists of *username* and *password*, which must be sent by Wget. As with HTTP authorization, several authentication schemes exist. For proxy authorization only the `Basic` authentication scheme is currently implemented.

You may specify your username and password either through the proxy URL or through the command-line options. Assuming that the company's proxy is located at '`proxy.company.com`' at port 8001, a proxy URL location containing authorization data might look like this:

    http://hniksic:mypassword@proxy.company.com:8001/

Alternatively, you may use the '`proxy-user`' and '`proxy-password`' options, and the equivalent `.wgetrc` settings `proxy_user` and `proxy_password` to set the proxy username and password.

8.2 Distribution

Like all GNU utilities, the latest version of Wget can be found at the master GNU archive site ftp.gnu.org, and its mirrors. For example, Wget 1.16.2 can be found at `ftp://ftp.gnu.org/pub/gnu/wget/wget-1.16.2.tar.gz`

8.3 Web Site

The official web site for GNU Wget is at `http://www.gnu.org/software/wget/`. However, most useful information resides at "The Wget Wgiki", `http://wget.addictivecode.org/`.

8.4 Mailing Lists

Primary List

The primary mailinglist for discussion, bug-reports, or questions about GNU Wget is at `bug-wget@gnu.org`. To subscribe, send an email to `bug-wget-join@gnu.org`, or visit `http://lists.gnu.org/mailman/listinfo/bug-wget`.

You do not need to subscribe to send a message to the list; however, please note that unsubscribed messages are moderated, and may take a while before they hit the list—**usually around a day**. If you want your message to show up immediately, please subscribe to the list before posting. Archives for the list may be found at `http://lists.gnu.org/pipermail/bug-wget/`.

An NNTP/Usenettish gateway is also available via Gmane. You can see the Gmane archives at `http://news.gmane.org/gmane.comp.web.wget.general`. Note that the Gmane archives conveniently include messages from both the current list, and the previous one. Messages also show up in the Gmane archives sooner than they do at `lists.gnu.org`.

Bug Notices List

Additionally, there is the `wget-notify@addictivecode.org` mailing list. This is a non-discussion list that receives bug report notifications from the bug-tracker. To subscribe to this list, send an email to `wget-notify-join@addictivecode.org`, or visit `http://addictivecode.org/mailman/listinfo/wget-notify`.

Obsolete Lists

Previously, the mailing list `wget@sunsite.dk` was used as the main discussion list, and another list, `wget-patches@sunsite.dk` was used for submitting and discussing patches to GNU Wget.

Messages from `wget@sunsite.dk` are archived at

`http://www.mail-archive.com/wget%40sunsite.dk/` and at

`http://news.gmane.org/gmane.comp.web.wget.general` (which also continues to archive the current list, `bug-wget@gnu.org`).

Messages from `wget-patches@sunsite.dk` are archived at

`http://news.gmane.org/gmane.comp.web.wget.patches`.

8.5 Internet Relay Chat

In addition to the mailinglists, we also have a support channel set up via IRC at `irc.freenode.org`, `#wget`. Come check it out!

8.6 Reporting Bugs

You are welcome to submit bug reports via the GNU Wget bug tracker (see `http://wget.addictivecode.org/BugTracker`).

Before actually submitting a bug report, please try to follow a few simple guidelines.

1. Please try to ascertain that the behavior you see really is a bug. If Wget crashes, it's a bug. If Wget does not behave as documented, it's a bug. If things work strange, but you are not sure about the way they are supposed to work, it might well be a bug, but you might want to double-check the documentation and the mailing lists (see Section 8.4 [Mailing Lists], page 50).

2. Try to repeat the bug in as simple circumstances as possible. E.g. if Wget crashes while downloading 'wget -r10 -kKE -t5 --no-proxy http://yoyodyne.com -o /tmp/log', you should try to see if the crash is repeatable, and if will occur with a simpler set of options. You might even try to start the download at the page where the crash occurred to see if that page somehow triggered the crash.

   Also, while I will probably be interested to know the contents of your .wgetrc file, just dumping it into the debug message is probably a bad idea. Instead, you should first try to see if the bug repeats with .wgetrc moved out of the way. Only if it turns out that .wgetrc settings affect the bug, mail me the relevant parts of the file.

3. Please start Wget with '-d' option and send us the resulting output (or relevant parts thereof). If Wget was compiled without debug support, recompile it it is *much* easier to trace bugs with debug support on.

   Note: please make sure to remove any potentially sensitive information from the debug log before sending it to the bug address. The -d won't go out of its way to collect sensitive information, but the log *will* contain a fairly complete transcript of Wget's communication with the server, which may include passwords and pieces of downloaded data. Since the bug address is publically archived, you may assume that all bug reports are visible to the public.

4. If Wget has crashed, try to run it in a debugger, e.g. gdb 'which wget' core and type where to get the backtrace. This may not work if the system administrator has disabled core files, but it is safe to try.

8.7 Portability

Like all GNU software, Wget works on the GNU system. However, since it uses GNU Autoconf for building and configuring, and mostly avoids using "special" features of any particular Unix, it should compile (and work) on all common Unix flavors.

Various Wget versions have been compiled and tested under many kinds of Unix systems, including GNU/Linux, Solaris, SunOS 4.x, Mac OS X, OSF (aka Digital Unix or Tru64), Ultrix, *BSD, IRIX, AIX, and others. Some of those systems are no longer in widespread use and may not be able to support recent versions of Wget. If Wget fails to compile on your system, we would like to know about it.

Thanks to kind contributors, this version of Wget compiles and works on 32-bit Microsoft Windows platforms. It has been compiled successfully using MS Visual C++ 6.0, Watcom, Borland C, and GCC compilers. Naturally, it is crippled of some features available on Unix, but it should work as a substitute for people stuck with Windows. Note that Windows-specific portions of Wget are not guaranteed to be supported in the future, although this has been the case in practice for many years now. All questions and problems in Windows usage should be reported to Wget mailing list at wget@sunsite.dk where the volunteers who maintain the Windows-related features might look at them.

Support for building on MS-DOS via DJGPP has been contributed by Gisle Vanem; a port to VMS is maintained by Steven Schweda, and is available at http://antinode.org/.

8.8 Signals

Since the purpose of Wget is background work, it catches the hangup signal (SIGHUP) and ignores it. If the output was on standard output, it will be redirected to a file named `wget-log`. Otherwise, SIGHUP is ignored. This is convenient when you wish to redirect the output of Wget after having started it.

```
$ wget http://www.gnus.org/dist/gnus.tar.gz &
...
$ kill -HUP %%
SIGHUP received, redirecting output to 'wget-log'.
```

Other than that, Wget will not try to interfere with signals in any way. *C-c*, `kill -TERM` and `kill -KILL` should kill it alike.

9 Appendices

This chapter contains some references I consider useful.

9.1 Robot Exclusion

It is extremely easy to make Wget wander aimlessly around a web site, sucking all the available data in progress. 'wget -r *site*', and you're set. Great? Not for the server admin.

As long as Wget is only retrieving static pages, and doing it at a reasonable rate (see the '--wait' option), there's not much of a problem. The trouble is that Wget can't tell the difference between the smallest static page and the most demanding CGI. A site I know has a section handled by a CGI Perl script that converts Info files to HTML on the fly. The script is slow, but works well enough for human users viewing an occasional Info file. However, when someone's recursive Wget download stumbles upon the index page that links to all the Info files through the script, the system is brought to its knees without providing anything useful to the user (This task of converting Info files could be done locally and access to Info documentation for all installed GNU software on a system is available from the info command).

To avoid this kind of accident, as well as to preserve privacy for documents that need to be protected from well-behaved robots, the concept of *robot exclusion* was invented. The idea is that the server administrators and document authors can specify which portions of the site they wish to protect from robots and those they will permit access.

The most popular mechanism, and the *de facto* standard supported by all the major robots, is the "Robots Exclusion Standard" (RES) written by Martijn Koster et al. in 1994. It specifies the format of a text file containing directives that instruct the robots which URL paths to avoid. To be found by the robots, the specifications must be placed in /robots.txt in the server root, which the robots are expected to download and parse.

Although Wget is not a web robot in the strictest sense of the word, it can download large parts of the site without the user's intervention to download an individual page. Because of that, Wget honors RES when downloading recursively. For instance, when you issue:

```
wget -r http://www.server.com/
```

First the index of 'www.server.com' will be downloaded. If Wget finds that it wants to download more documents from that server, it will request 'http://www.server.com/robots.txt' and, if found, use it for further downloads. robots.txt is loaded only once per each server.

Until version 1.8, Wget supported the first version of the standard, written by Martijn Koster in 1994 and available at http://www.robotstxt.org/wc/norobots.html. As of version 1.8, Wget has supported the additional directives specified in the internet draft '<draft-koster-robots-00.txt>' titled "A Method for Web Robots Control". The draft, which has as far as I know never made to an RFC, is available at http://www.robotstxt.org/wc/norobots-rfc.txt.

This manual no longer includes the text of the Robot Exclusion Standard.

The second, less known mechanism, enables the author of an individual document to specify whether they want the links from the file to be followed by a robot. This is achieved using the META tag, like this:

```
<meta name="robots" content="nofollow">
```

This is explained in some detail at http://www.robotstxt.org/wc/meta-user.html. Wget supports this method of robot exclusion in addition to the usual /robots.txt exclusion.

If you know what you are doing and really really wish to turn off the robot exclusion, set the robots variable to 'off' in your .wgetrc. You can achieve the same effect from the command line using the -e switch, e.g. 'wget -e robots=off *url*...'.

9.2 Security Considerations

When using Wget, you must be aware that it sends unencrypted passwords through the network, which may present a security problem. Here are the main issues, and some solutions.

1. The passwords on the command line are visible using `ps`. The best way around it is to use `wget -i -` and feed the URLs to Wget's standard input, each on a separate line, terminated by *C-d*. Another workaround is to use `.netrc` to store passwords; however, storing unencrypted passwords is also considered a security risk.

2. Using the insecure *basic* authentication scheme, unencrypted passwords are transmitted through the network routers and gateways.

3. The FTP passwords are also in no way encrypted. There is no good solution for this at the moment.

4. Although the "normal" output of Wget tries to hide the passwords, debugging logs show them, in all forms. This problem is avoided by being careful when you send debug logs (yes, even when you send them to me).

9.3 Contributors

GNU Wget was written by Hrvoje Nikšić `hniksic@xemacs.org`,

However, the development of Wget could never have gone as far as it has, were it not for the help of many people, either with bug reports, feature proposals, patches, or letters saying "Thanks!".

Special thanks goes to the following people (no particular order):

- Dan Harkless—contributed a lot of code and documentation of extremely high quality, as well as the `--page-requisites` and related options. He was the principal maintainer for some time and released Wget 1.6.

- Ian Abbott—contributed bug fixes, Windows-related fixes, and provided a prototype implementation of the breadth-first recursive download. Co-maintained Wget during the 1.8 release cycle.

- The dotsrc.org crew, in particular Karsten Thygesen—donated system resources such as the mailing list, web space, FTP space, and version control repositories, along with a lot of time to make these actually work. Christian Reiniger was of invaluable help with setting up Subversion.

- Heiko Herold—provided high-quality Windows builds and contributed bug and build reports for many years.

- Shawn McHorse—bug reports and patches.

- Kaveh R. Ghazi—on-the-fly `ansi2knr`-ization. Lots of portability fixes.

- Gordon Matzigkeit—`.netrc` support.

- Zlatko Čalušić, Tomislav Vujec and Dražen Kačar—feature suggestions and "philosophical" discussions.

- Darko Budor—initial port to Windows.

- Antonio Rosella—help and suggestions, plus the initial Italian translation.

- Tomislav Petrović, Mario Mikočević—many bug reports and suggestions.

- François Pinard—many thorough bug reports and discussions.

- Karl Eichwalder—lots of help with internationalization, Makefile layout and many other things.

- Junio Hamano—donated support for Opie and HTTP `Digest` authentication.

- Mauro Tortonesi—improved IPv6 support, adding support for dual family systems. Refactored and enhanced FTP IPv6 code. Maintained GNU Wget from 2004–2007.

- Christopher G. Lewis—maintenance of the Windows version of GNU WGet.
- Gisle Vanem—many helpful patches and improvements, especially for Windows and MS-DOS support.
- Ralf Wildenhues—contributed patches to convert Wget to use Automake as part of its build process, and various bugfixes.
- Steven Schubiger—Many helpful patches, bugfixes and improvements. Notably, conversion of Wget to use the Gnulib quotes and quotearqs modules, and the addition of password prompts at the console, via the Gnulib getpasswd-gnu module.
- Ted Mielczarek—donated support for CSS.
- Saint Xavier—Support for IRIs (RFC 3987).
- People who provided donations for development—including Brian Gough.

The following people have provided patches, bug/build reports, useful suggestions, beta testing services, fan mail and all the other things that make maintenance so much fun:

Tim Adam, Adrian Aichner, Martin Baehr, Dieter Baron, Roger Beeman, Dan Berger, T. Bharath, Christian Biere, Paul Bludov, Daniel Bodea, Mark Boyns, John Burden, Julien Buty, Wanderlei Cavassin, Gilles Cedoc, Tim Charron, Noel Cragg, Kristijan Čonkaš, John Daily, Andreas Damm, Ahmon Dancy, Andrew Davison, Bertrand Demiddelaer, Alexander Dergachev, Andrew Deryabin, Ulrich Drepper, Marc Duponcheel, Damir Džeko, Alan Eldridge, Hans-Andreas Engel, Aleksandar Erkalović, Andy Eskilsson, Joao Ferreira, Christian Fraenkel, David Fritz, Mike Frysinger, Charles C. Fu, FUJISHIMA Satsuki, Masashi Fujita, Howard Gayle, Marcel Gerrits, Lemble Gregory, Hans Grobler, Alain Guibert, Mathieu Guillaume, Aaron Hawley, Jochen Hein, Karl Heuer, Madhusudan Hosaagrahara, HIROSE Masaaki, Ulf Harnhammar, Gregor Hoffleit, Erik Magnus Hulthen, Richard Huveneers, Jonas Jensen, Larry Jones, Simon Josefsson, Mario Jurić, Hack Kampbjørn, Const Kaplinsky, Goran Kezunović, Igor Khristophorov, Robert Kleine, KOJIMA Haime, Fila Kolodny, Alexander Kourakos, Martin Kraemer, Sami Krank, Jay Krell, Σίμος Ξενιτέλλης (Simos KSenitellis), Christian Lackas, Hrvoje Lacko, Daniel S. Lewart, Nicolás Lichtmeier, Dave Love, Alexander V. Lukyanov, Thomas Lußnig, Andre Majorel, Aurelien Marchand, Matthew J. Mellon, Jordan Mendelson, Ted Mielczarek, Robert Millan, Lin Zhe Min, Jan Minar, Tim Mooney, Keith Moore, Adam D. Moss, Simon Munton, Charlie Negyesi, R. K. Owen, Jim Paris, Kenny Parnell, Leonid Petrov, Simone Piunno, Andrew Pollock, Steve Pothier, Jan Přikryl, Marin Purgar, Csaba Ráduly, Keith Refson, Bill Richardson, Tyler Riddle, Tobias Ringstrom, Jochen Roderburg, Juan José Rodríguez, Maciej W. Rozycki, Edward J. Sabol, Heinz Salzmann, Robert Schmidt, Nicolas Schodet, Benno Schulenberg, Andreas Schwab, Steven M. Schweda, Chris Seawood, Pranab Shenoy, Dennis Smit, Toomas Soome, Tage Stabell-Kulo, Philip Stadermann, Daniel Stenberg, Sven Sternberger, Markus Strasser, John Summerfield, Szakacsits Szabolcs, Mike Thomas, Philipp Thomas, Mauro Tortonesi, Dave Turner, Gisle Vanem, Rabin Vincent, Russell Vincent, Željko Vrba, Charles G Waldman, Douglas E. Wegscheid, Ralf Wildenhues, Joshua David Williams, Benjamin Wolsey, Saint Xavier, YAMAZAKI Makoto, Jasmin Zainul, Bojan Ždrnja, Kristijan Zimmer, Xin Zou.

Apologies to all who I accidentally left out, and many thanks to all the subscribers of the Wget mailing list.

Appendix A Copying this manual

A.1 GNU Free Documentation License

Version 1.3, 3 November 2008

Copyright © 2000, 2001, 2002, 2007, 2008 Free Software Foundation, Inc.
`http://fsf.org/`

Everyone is permitted to copy and distribute verbatim copies
of this license document, but changing it is not allowed.

0. PREAMBLE

The purpose of this License is to make a manual, textbook, or other functional and useful document *free* in the sense of freedom: to assure everyone the effective freedom to copy and redistribute it, with or without modifying it, either commercially or noncommercially. Secondarily, this License preserves for the author and publisher a way to get credit for their work, while not being considered responsible for modifications made by others.

This License is a kind of "copyleft", which means that derivative works of the document must themselves be free in the same sense. It complements the GNU General Public License, which is a copyleft license designed for free software.

We have designed this License in order to use it for manuals for free software, because free software needs free documentation: a free program should come with manuals providing the same freedoms that the software does. But this License is not limited to software manuals; it can be used for any textual work, regardless of subject matter or whether it is published as a printed book. We recommend this License principally for works whose purpose is instruction or reference.

1. APPLICABILITY AND DEFINITIONS

This License applies to any manual or other work, in any medium, that contains a notice placed by the copyright holder saying it can be distributed under the terms of this License. Such a notice grants a world-wide, royalty-free license, unlimited in duration, to use that work under the conditions stated herein. The "Document", below, refers to any such manual or work. Any member of the public is a licensee, and is addressed as "you". You accept the license if you copy, modify or distribute the work in a way requiring permission under copyright law.

A "Modified Version" of the Document means any work containing the Document or a portion of it, either copied verbatim, or with modifications and/or translated into another language.

A "Secondary Section" is a named appendix or a front-matter section of the Document that deals exclusively with the relationship of the publishers or authors of the Document to the Document's overall subject (or to related matters) and contains nothing that could fall directly within that overall subject. (Thus, if the Document is in part a textbook of mathematics, a Secondary Section may not explain any mathematics.) The relationship could be a matter of historical connection with the subject or with related matters, or of legal, commercial, philosophical, ethical or political position regarding them.

The "Invariant Sections" are certain Secondary Sections whose titles are designated, as being those of Invariant Sections, in the notice that says that the Document is released under this License. If a section does not fit the above definition of Secondary then it is not allowed to be designated as Invariant. The Document may contain zero Invariant Sections. If the Document does not identify any Invariant Sections then there are none.

The "Cover Texts" are certain short passages of text that are listed, as Front-Cover Texts or Back-Cover Texts, in the notice that says that the Document is released under this License.

A Front-Cover Text may be at most 5 words, and a Back-Cover Text may be at most 25 words.

A "Transparent" copy of the Document means a machine-readable copy, represented in a format whose specification is available to the general public, that is suitable for revising the document straightforwardly with generic text editors or (for images composed of pixels) generic paint programs or (for drawings) some widely available drawing editor, and that is suitable for input to text formatters or for automatic translation to a variety of formats suitable for input to text formatters. A copy made in an otherwise Transparent file format whose markup, or absence of markup, has been arranged to thwart or discourage subsequent modification by readers is not Transparent. An image format is not Transparent if used for any substantial amount of text. A copy that is not "Transparent" is called "Opaque".

Examples of suitable formats for Transparent copies include plain ASCII without markup, Texinfo input format, LaTeX input format, SGML or XML using a publicly available DTD, and standard-conforming simple HTML, PostScript or PDF designed for human modification. Examples of transparent image formats include PNG, XCF and JPG. Opaque formats include proprietary formats that can be read and edited only by proprietary word processors, SGML or XML for which the DTD and/or processing tools are not generally available, and the machine-generated HTML, PostScript or PDF produced by some word processors for output purposes only.

The "Title Page" means, for a printed book, the title page itself, plus such following pages as are needed to hold, legibly, the material this License requires to appear in the title page. For works in formats which do not have any title page as such, "Title Page" means the text near the most prominent appearance of the work's title, preceding the beginning of the body of the text.

The "publisher" means any person or entity that distributes copies of the Document to the public.

A section "Entitled XYZ" means a named subunit of the Document whose title either is precisely XYZ or contains XYZ in parentheses following text that translates XYZ in another language. (Here XYZ stands for a specific section name mentioned below, such as "Acknowledgements", "Dedications", "Endorsements", or "History".) To "Preserve the Title" of such a section when you modify the Document means that it remains a section "Entitled XYZ" according to this definition.

The Document may include Warranty Disclaimers next to the notice which states that this License applies to the Document. These Warranty Disclaimers are considered to be included by reference in this License, but only as regards disclaiming warranties: any other implication that these Warranty Disclaimers may have is void and has no effect on the meaning of this License.

2. VERBATIM COPYING

You may copy and distribute the Document in any medium, either commercially or noncommercially, provided that this License, the copyright notices, and the license notice saying this License applies to the Document are reproduced in all copies, and that you add no other conditions whatsoever to those of this License. You may not use technical measures to obstruct or control the reading or further copying of the copies you make or distribute. However, you may accept compensation in exchange for copies. If you distribute a large enough number of copies you must also follow the conditions in section 3.

You may also lend copies, under the same conditions stated above, and you may publicly display copies.

3. COPYING IN QUANTITY

If you publish printed copies (or copies in media that commonly have printed covers) of the Document, numbering more than 100, and the Document's license notice requires Cover

Texts, you must enclose the copies in covers that carry, clearly and legibly, all these Cover Texts: Front-Cover Texts on the front cover, and Back-Cover Texts on the back cover. Both covers must also clearly and legibly identify you as the publisher of these copies. The front cover must present the full title with all words of the title equally prominent and visible. You may add other material on the covers in addition. Copying with changes limited to the covers, as long as they preserve the title of the Document and satisfy these conditions, can be treated as verbatim copying in other respects.

If the required texts for either cover are too voluminous to fit legibly, you should put the first ones listed (as many as fit reasonably) on the actual cover, and continue the rest onto adjacent pages.

If you publish or distribute Opaque copies of the Document numbering more than 100, you must either include a machine-readable Transparent copy along with each Opaque copy, or state in or with each Opaque copy a computer-network location from which the general network-using public has access to download using public-standard network protocols a complete Transparent copy of the Document, free of added material. If you use the latter option, you must take reasonably prudent steps, when you begin distribution of Opaque copies in quantity, to ensure that this Transparent copy will remain thus accessible at the stated location until at least one year after the last time you distribute an Opaque copy (directly or through your agents or retailers) of that edition to the public.

It is requested, but not required, that you contact the authors of the Document well before redistributing any large number of copies, to give them a chance to provide you with an updated version of the Document.

4. MODIFICATIONS

You may copy and distribute a Modified Version of the Document under the conditions of sections 2 and 3 above, provided that you release the Modified Version under precisely this License, with the Modified Version filling the role of the Document, thus licensing distribution and modification of the Modified Version to whoever possesses a copy of it. In addition, you must do these things in the Modified Version:

A. Use in the Title Page (and on the covers, if any) a title distinct from that of the Document, and from those of previous versions (which should, if there were any, be listed in the History section of the Document). You may use the same title as a previous version if the original publisher of that version gives permission.

B. List on the Title Page, as authors, one or more persons or entities responsible for authorship of the modifications in the Modified Version, together with at least five of the principal authors of the Document (all of its principal authors, if it has fewer than five), unless they release you from this requirement.

C. State on the Title page the name of the publisher of the Modified Version, as the publisher.

D. Preserve all the copyright notices of the Document.

E. Add an appropriate copyright notice for your modifications adjacent to the other copyright notices.

F. Include, immediately after the copyright notices, a license notice giving the public permission to use the Modified Version under the terms of this License, in the form shown in the Addendum below.

G. Preserve in that license notice the full lists of Invariant Sections and required Cover Texts given in the Document's license notice.

H. Include an unaltered copy of this License.

I. Preserve the section Entitled "History", Preserve its Title, and add to it an item stating at least the title, year, new authors, and publisher of the Modified Version as given on the Title Page. If there is no section Entitled "History" in the Document, create one stating the title, year, authors, and publisher of the Document as given on its Title Page, then add an item describing the Modified Version as stated in the previous sentence.

J. Preserve the network location, if any, given in the Document for public access to a Transparent copy of the Document, and likewise the network locations given in the Document for previous versions it was based on. These may be placed in the "History" section. You may omit a network location for a work that was published at least four years before the Document itself, or if the original publisher of the version it refers to gives permission.

K. For any section Entitled "Acknowledgements" or "Dedications", Preserve the Title of the section, and preserve in the section all the substance and tone of each of the contributor acknowledgements and/or dedications given therein.

L. Preserve all the Invariant Sections of the Document, unaltered in their text and in their titles. Section numbers or the equivalent are not considered part of the section titles.

M. Delete any section Entitled "Endorsements". Such a section may not be included in the Modified Version.

N. Do not retitle any existing section to be Entitled "Endorsements" or to conflict in title with any Invariant Section.

O. Preserve any Warranty Disclaimers.

If the Modified Version includes new front-matter sections or appendices that qualify as Secondary Sections and contain no material copied from the Document, you may at your option designate some or all of these sections as invariant. To do this, add their titles to the list of Invariant Sections in the Modified Version's license notice. These titles must be distinct from any other section titles.

You may add a section Entitled "Endorsements", provided it contains nothing but endorsements of your Modified Version by various parties—for example, statements of peer review or that the text has been approved by an organization as the authoritative definition of a standard.

You may add a passage of up to five words as a Front-Cover Text, and a passage of up to 25 words as a Back-Cover Text, to the end of the list of Cover Texts in the Modified Version. Only one passage of Front-Cover Text and one of Back-Cover Text may be added by (or through arrangements made by) any one entity. If the Document already includes a cover text for the same cover, previously added by you or by arrangement made by the same entity you are acting on behalf of, you may not add another; but you may replace the old one, on explicit permission from the previous publisher that added the old one.

The author(s) and publisher(s) of the Document do not by this License give permission to use their names for publicity for or to assert or imply endorsement of any Modified Version.

5. COMBINING DOCUMENTS

You may combine the Document with other documents released under this License, under the terms defined in section 4 above for modified versions, provided that you include in the combination all of the Invariant Sections of all of the original documents, unmodified, and list them all as Invariant Sections of your combined work in its license notice, and that you preserve all their Warranty Disclaimers.

The combined work need only contain one copy of this License, and multiple identical Invariant Sections may be replaced with a single copy. If there are multiple Invariant Sections with the same name but different contents, make the title of each such section unique by adding at the end of it, in parentheses, the name of the original author or publisher of that section if known, or else a unique number. Make the same adjustment to the section titles in the list of Invariant Sections in the license notice of the combined work.

In the combination, you must combine any sections Entitled "History" in the various original documents, forming one section Entitled "History"; likewise combine any sections Entitled "Acknowledgements", and any sections Entitled "Dedications". You must delete all sections Entitled "Endorsements."

6. COLLECTIONS OF DOCUMENTS

You may make a collection consisting of the Document and other documents released under this License, and replace the individual copies of this License in the various documents with a single copy that is included in the collection, provided that you follow the rules of this License for verbatim copying of each of the documents in all other respects.

You may extract a single document from such a collection, and distribute it individually under this License, provided you insert a copy of this License into the extracted document, and follow this License in all other respects regarding verbatim copying of that document.

7. AGGREGATION WITH INDEPENDENT WORKS

A compilation of the Document or its derivatives with other separate and independent documents or works, in or on a volume of a storage or distribution medium, is called an "aggregate" if the copyright resulting from the compilation is not used to limit the legal rights of the compilation's users beyond what the individual works permit. When the Document is included in an aggregate, this License does not apply to the other works in the aggregate which are not themselves derivative works of the Document.

If the Cover Text requirement of section 3 is applicable to these copies of the Document, then if the Document is less than one half of the entire aggregate, the Document's Cover Texts may be placed on covers that bracket the Document within the aggregate, or the electronic equivalent of covers if the Document is in electronic form. Otherwise they must appear on printed covers that bracket the whole aggregate.

8. TRANSLATION

Translation is considered a kind of modification, so you may distribute translations of the Document under the terms of section 4. Replacing Invariant Sections with translations requires special permission from their copyright holders, but you may include translations of some or all Invariant Sections in addition to the original versions of these Invariant Sections. You may include a translation of this License, and all the license notices in the Document, and any Warranty Disclaimers, provided that you also include the original English version of this License and the original versions of those notices and disclaimers. In case of a disagreement between the translation and the original version of this License or a notice or disclaimer, the original version will prevail.

If a section in the Document is Entitled "Acknowledgements", "Dedications", or "History", the requirement (section 4) to Preserve its Title (section 1) will typically require changing the actual title.

9. TERMINATION

You may not copy, modify, sublicense, or distribute the Document except as expressly provided under this License. Any attempt otherwise to copy, modify, sublicense, or distribute it is void, and will automatically terminate your rights under this License.

However, if you cease all violation of this License, then your license from a particular copyright holder is reinstated (a) provisionally, unless and until the copyright holder explicitly and finally terminates your license, and (b) permanently, if the copyright holder fails to notify you of the violation by some reasonable means prior to 60 days after the cessation.

Moreover, your license from a particular copyright holder is reinstated permanently if the copyright holder notifies you of the violation by some reasonable means, this is the first time you have received notice of violation of this License (for any work) from that copyright holder, and you cure the violation prior to 30 days after your receipt of the notice.

Termination of your rights under this section does not terminate the licenses of parties who have received copies or rights from you under this License. If your rights have been terminated and not permanently reinstated, receipt of a copy of some or all of the same material does not give you any rights to use it.

10. FUTURE REVISIONS OF THIS LICENSE

The Free Software Foundation may publish new, revised versions of the GNU Free Documentation License from time to time. Such new versions will be similar in spirit to the present version, but may differ in detail to address new problems or concerns. See `http://www.gnu.org/copyleft/`.

Each version of the License is given a distinguishing version number. If the Document specifies that a particular numbered version of this License "or any later version" applies to it, you have the option of following the terms and conditions either of that specified version or of any later version that has been published (not as a draft) by the Free Software Foundation. If the Document does not specify a version number of this License, you may choose any version ever published (not as a draft) by the Free Software Foundation. If the Document specifies that a proxy can decide which future versions of this License can be used, that proxy's public statement of acceptance of a version permanently authorizes you to choose that version for the Document.

11. RELICENSING

"Massive Multiauthor Collaboration Site" (or "MMC Site") means any World Wide Web server that publishes copyrightable works and also provides prominent facilities for anybody to edit those works. A public wiki that anybody can edit is an example of such a server. A "Massive Multiauthor Collaboration" (or "MMC") contained in the site means any set of copyrightable works thus published on the MMC site.

"CC-BY-SA" means the Creative Commons Attribution-Share Alike 3.0 license published by Creative Commons Corporation, a not-for-profit corporation with a principal place of business in San Francisco, California, as well as future copyleft versions of that license published by that same organization.

"Incorporate" means to publish or republish a Document, in whole or in part, as part of another Document.

An MMC is "eligible for relicensing" if it is licensed under this License, and if all works that were first published under this License somewhere other than this MMC, and subsequently incorporated in whole or in part into the MMC, (1) had no cover texts or invariant sections, and (2) were thus incorporated prior to November 1, 2008.

The operator of an MMC Site may republish an MMC contained in the site under CC-BY-SA on the same site at any time before August 1, 2009, provided the MMC is eligible for relicensing.

ADDENDUM: How to use this License for your documents

To use this License in a document you have written, include a copy of the License in the document and put the following copyright and license notices just after the title page:

```
Copyright (C)  year  your name.
Permission is granted to copy, distribute and/or modify this document
under the terms of the GNU Free Documentation License, Version 1.3
or any later version published by the Free Software Foundation;
with no Invariant Sections, no Front-Cover Texts, and no Back-Cover
Texts.  A copy of the license is included in the section entitled ''GNU
Free Documentation License''.
```

If you have Invariant Sections, Front-Cover Texts and Back-Cover Texts, replace the "with. . . Texts." line with this:

```
with the Invariant Sections being list their titles, with
the Front-Cover Texts being list, and with the Back-Cover Texts
being list.
```

If you have Invariant Sections without Cover Texts, or some other combination of the three, merge those two alternatives to suit the situation.

If your document contains nontrivial examples of program code, we recommend releasing these examples in parallel under your choice of free software license, such as the GNU General Public License, to permit their use in free software.

Concept Index

Table of Contents

www.ingramcontent.com/pod-product-compliance
Lightning Source LLC
LaVergne TN
LVHW060148070326
832902LV00018B/3003